The Hidden
Lives of Seven
Teen Girls

PERFECTLYSECRET

annick press
toronto+new york+vancouver

Text © 2004 Introduction, Susan Musgrave; "Truth, Dare, Kiss, Command, or Promise: Fragments from a Life," Cathy Stonehouse; "The Damsite," Nan Germaine; "Unseen, Unheard," Kelys Green; "Cherry Pride," Susan Musgrave; "Mad as Sheela," Anita Rau Badami; "Dancing with My Father," Lorna Crozier; "There Will Be No Secrets," Almeda Glenn Miller

Second printing, February 2009

We acknowledge the support of the Canada Council for the Arts, the Ontario Arts Council, and the Government of Canada through the Book Publishing Industry Development Program (BPIDP) for our publishing activities.

 ONTARIO ARTS COUNCIL
CONSEIL DES ARTS DE L'ONTARIO

Edited by Barbara Pulling
Copy-edited by Elizabeth McLean
Cover and interior design by Irvin Cheung/iCheung Design
Cover photograph by Sean Justice/The Image Bank/Getty Images

The text was typeset in Bembo and Trade Gothic

Cataloging in Publication

Perfectly secret : the hidden lives of seven teen girls / edited by Susan Musgrave.

ISBN 1-55037-865-1 (bound).—ISBN 1-55037-864-3 (pbk.)

    1. Teenage girls. I. Musgrave, Susan, 1951-

HQ798.P47 2004   305.235'082   C2004-902218-0

Printed and bound in Canada

Distributed in Canada by	**Distributed in the U.S.A. by**	**Published in the U.S.A. by**
Firefly Books Ltd.	Firefly Books (U.S.) Inc.	Annick Press (U.S.) Ltd.
66 Leek Crescent	P.O. Box 1338	
Richmond Hill, ON	Ellicott Station	
L4B 1H1	Buffalo, NY 14205	

visit us at **www.annickpress.com**
visit Susan Musgrave at **www.susanmusgrave.com**

To see excerpts from other books in this series, please turn to p.98.

Contents

Introduction

WE ALL KEEP SECRETS. We keep secrets because we are embarrassed or afraid. We keep secrets so we won't get into trouble or bring down the heat on somebody else. Sometimes we keep secrets for other people, too. Friends, or even parents, may trust us with secrets we wish we didn't know, and their secrets can become our burdens.

When I was fifteen, my best friend told me she wanted to kill herself, and she made me promise not to tell anyone about her plan. I was afraid that if I didn't tell someone and she succeeded, I would be responsible. I was afraid, too, that if I broke my promise to her and *did* get help, she would never trust me again and would stop being my friend.

Many of the stories in this collection are concerned in some way or another with the keeping of family secrets. In Nan Germaine's essay, "The Damsite," a mother confides in her daughter because she has no one else she can talk to. "My secrets were not exactly my own: they were the secrets of others," Nan writes. "They were the confessions my mother made to me about her unhappiness. They were the actions of my father, which I observed when he took me with him on his business trips." Being privy to her parents' secrets makes Nan feel important at first, but as she gets older she comes to resent it.

Sometimes we keep secrets because we fear for our safety. Kelys Green still has a scar on her breast from where she collided with a doorknob while her father was chasing her with a wooden coat hanger. Although she later came to understand that her parents loved her the best way they knew how, the pain of her early experiences remained. "He beat me until the hanger broke," she writes, with heartbreaking clarity and simplicity. "What was the big secret in my world? *I* was. Anything I was thinking or feeling, I kept to myself."

We sometimes keep secrets for the same reason we may tell lies—to protect those we love from getting hurt, even though their actions have hurt us, over and over again. "Having to lie is a burden, but the worst effect of our secret is that it forces me to hide my sadness," Lorna Crozier writes about her father's alcoholism. Shame, she says, was a large part of living with him. "What our secret means... is that I can't invite my friends home after school or ask them to stay for supper... I can't tell anyone the real reason why Mom and I walk everywhere: Dad's too inebriated to drive."

Anita Rau Badami writes about feelings of shame as

well—for a crazy aunt, her father's sister, who is madness personified: "Sheela was our shameful secret... If people knew we had a lunatic for an aunt, they might not want to be acquainted with us, my mother said ominously." Unless Anita keeps the secret, her mother tells her, no one will marry her, or give anyone in the family a job, or even get close to them, "just in case the madness that ran in our family had infected us."

We also keep secrets to protect our freedom, so we can continue to experiment without rocking, or capsizing, the proverbial boat at home. When Almeda Glenn Miller and her brothers experiment with drugs, they don't discuss it with their father, or the social worker, but their mother knows—and even says "she wants to try smoking marijuana with us sometime." "For my mom," Almeda writes, "secrets are the horrible dark things that selfish people whisper behind closed doors. They are the dangerous breeding grounds for deception." Her mother even removes the lock on the bathroom door, declaring, "There will be no secrets in this family." And yet, there are always secrets.

Perhaps our darkest secrets are those we conceal from ourselves. Sometimes the abuse or pain we suffer can be so great that we feel we have no choice but to hide from it. Cathy Stonehouse writes about this in her story, "Truth, Dare, Kiss, Command, or Promise": "Keeping other people's secrets may be difficult, but sharing her own is altogether impossible..."

One of the saddest things about secrets is that we use them to present ourselves the way we *think* others want to see us, when in fact most people are capable of seeing us, and accepting us, just as we are. If we're lucky, we'll discover this for ourselves and won't remain hostages to our secrets.

—Susan Musgrave

Truth, Dare, Kiss, Command, or Promise: Fragments from a Life

Cathy Stonehouse

Fragment One: Now You See Me, Now You Don't

MEET CATHY, my public personality. It's a Wednesday lunchtime, almost the end of our school year, and she's sitting on a desk in our stinky form room, hunched over a dog-eared copy of *The Lord of the Rings, Book Three*. Like me, she is white-skinned, black-haired, five-foot-six, and has just turned fourteen. Like me, she is munching on a squashed cottage cheese and cucumber sandwich. Unlike me, she is innocent and pure.

Sometimes Cathy answers questions, laughs (in case anyone doubts she has a sense of humor), or cracks a joke at her own expense. Otherwise, while her classmates talk, giggle, swear, swap makeup and shoes, do quizzes out of magazines, and impersonate teachers, she keeps her mouth shut, tries not to fidget, and reads.

That's because she knows I'm here. The part of her that

knows awful things she doesn't. I make her anxious. And the reason I'm here is because one of the other girls sitting around the form room has just suggested playing Cathy's least favorite game.

Here's how it goes. You ask someone to do something really disgusting—touch a piece of dog shit, say, or eat half a worm—or extremely painful—let someone else give her a wrist burn—and the person has to either do it or pick one of life's five options: Truth, Dare, Kiss, Command, or Promise. If she picks Truth, she has to answer a question truthfully. If she picks Dare, she gets given another hideous test. Picking Kiss results in an order to kiss someone (or something). Picking Command results in an order the person has to obey; picking Promise in a vow she has to keep.

When Cathy was younger, she was better at this game. She has quite a reputation for withstanding pain. If you ask her to stick her fingers in boiling water or pierce the skin between her toes with a needle, she'll go ahead and do it. Doing disgusting things is also easy for her. So often she didn't even have to choose.

But lately the tasks have become more difficult: tell Mr. Roberts (our Religious Education teacher) you want to have sex with him; go up to that man in the leather jacket and ask him out; describe your boyfriend's penis. Etcetera. The kinds of things that only *I* know about.

"Are you playing, Cathy?"

A chill runs up Cathy's spine. She's not in the mood for playing games. Keeping other people's secrets may be difficult, but sharing her own is altogether impossible, given that she doesn't have a clue what they actually are. As for kissing anything, well, that's my department. No, she's feeling decidedly nervous and spaced-out today; it really wouldn't be a good idea to join in.

So she shakes her head, buries her nose deep in her book, and loses herself in another, parallel universe. One she enters with relief, like Frodo pushing his finger through the Dark Lord's ring.

Reading is wonderful, exciting yet calming. Still, part of Cathy feels sad and lonely, wishes she could play along with the others, wishes she could understand what lies behind this familiar sensation of embarrassment, yuckiness, guilt, and dread.

Fragment Two: Cross My Heart and Hope To Die

CATHY AND I DO SHARE SOME SECRETS. For example, there is a man whose name Cathy is never, ever to mention in front of her dad. On pain of death, Cathy's mother says. Although this is never spoken, Cathy understands that her mum once had an affair with this man. When Cathy's dad says that the decorative knife he keeps hanging by the front door is there in case a certain bad man turns up on the doorstep, in which case he will slit the bad man's throat, Cathy must pretend she isn't scared. And when Cathy's dad asks her, in front of Cathy's mum, whether she knows what "adultery" means, and whether, in her opinion, adultery is bad, Cathy must swallow her fear and act like she doesn't have a clue what her father is talking about. Even though she does. And her father knows she does. The whole conversation, as everyone present is all too well aware, is being staged for the benefit of Cathy's mother, in order to let her know that he knows that Cathy knows. The gravity of the situation is underlined by the fact that Cathy's dad just happens, at that particular moment, to be cleaning his decorative knife at the kitchen table. Polishing it, sharpening up its blade.

Welcome to Cathy's home life.

What Cathy *doesn't* know is that there is another layer to this secret. Cathy's dad is also having a kind of affair. The person he is having the "affair" with, the "other woman," has herself been threatened with the decorative knife, has been told that Cathy's dad will slit *her* throat (and her mother's, while he is at it) should she ever tell on him. The "affair" has been going on ever since Cathy was little. She has learned that there's nothing whatsoever she can do to stop it. If she walked around thinking about it, *knowing* about it, she would go stark raving mad.

Fragment Three: Go to Your Room

SOMETIMES CATHY JUST STARTS SCREAMING. Not when she's at school, but when she's at home. She feels so incredibly angry. So angry at her mother. Sometimes she tells her mother to fuck off. If it's dinnertime, and she and her brother and parents are sitting round the dining-room table, her father will tell her to go upstairs to her room.

If he's talking to her, that is. Cathy's dad regularly stops talking to the members of his family, one at a time, for weeks on end. Nobody ever finds out why.

In her room Cathy will play records and sing along to them, the lyrics speaking for her. *Pressure,* sings David Bowie. *Pressing down on me, pressing down on you.* Or she will sit and sulk and listen to her parents arguing downstairs: *If we ever separate,* her father predicts, *it'll be over that child.*

That child. From the way her father says this, Cathy has deduced that she is bad, that there's something vile and unmentionable about her. Her mother has implied as much when exclaiming over Cathy's dirty knickers, how she has to boil them hard to get the stains out. Cathy's mother constantly reminds Cathy not to let her legs fall apart when sitting down in public and not to leave the curtains open when she gets undressed for bed. Girls who do those things are asking for it.

"Asking for what?" asks Cathy, although she knows the answer.

Asking to get raped.

Except she already has been. She doesn't know this, but I do. And like me, this knowledge lives in Cathy like a dormant disease. For example, on certain mornings Cathy wakes wondering how the man, half-remembered, got into her room the night before. Then blinks and wonders what on earth she is thinking about. Gets up, unfolds her school clothes, and carries on.

Fragment Four: How Did You Learn To Kiss Like That?

CATHY HAS NEVER HAD A PROPER BOYFRIEND. She feels terrible about this, convinced there is something wrong with her, some reason she is unlovable. But the fact is, she does her best to avoid all men and boys. At night she fantasizes about having sex with TV actors, pop stars, and professional athletes. These fantasies make her feel anxious sometimes, especially when the man's naked body comes into focus. Because no matter how she tries to make it look different, his body always looks exactly the same. Like a body she is being forced up against. A body she can only look at in close-up, so that its characteristics remain disconnected, reassuringly strange.

Once, at a village disco, Cathy found herself kissing and groping a much older boy. It was really embarrassing. One minute she was frozen, terrified, unable to speak a word while he roughly touched her, the next he was pulling away himself, gasping for air. What was the matter with him, wondered Cathy, and why was everyone suddenly staring at her?

No one in her family touches, if they can avoid it. She's never seen her parents kiss, and if her mum tries to hug her dad he stiffens into a statue and looks away, expressionless. But sometimes, on weekend mornings, Cathy's mum will come into her room and slide into bed with her, asking for hugs. "You know your father isn't very affectionate," she says to Cathy. Cathy acts like her dad then, stiffening up and looking away, convinced the flash in her mother's eyes is accusatory. As if all words in this house have a double meaning. *It'll be over that child.*

Fragment Five: I Dare You To Open Your Eyes

SOMETIMES, WHEN CATHY LOOKS AT HERSELF in the mirror, she catches a glimpse of me: the bad person, the awful person, the one who does the things Cathy doesn't want to. The one who opens her eyes when Cathy closes hers. Sometimes, in the evening, Cathy slows a little as she passes the mirror and sees a girl looking back: a girl who somehow isn't her, a girl just getting ready to start her day.

"Do you want to come for a walk?" asks a friend, calling round in the evening.

"No," says Cathy, terrified suddenly. Who knows what might happen, out there in the dark. "I'm really tired. I have to go to bed."

It's hard to be adventurous when you're scared all the time. Living in Cathy's house is like living on a tectonic fault line: you never know when the earth will start shuddering beneath you and the fragile shelter you've erected come tumbling down. One minute her dad is joking around hysterically, placing a vase upside down on his head and pretending he is a Roman soldier, or grimacing and clutching his crotch as if he's caught his penis in the sliding doors. The next he is exploding with rage and bitterness. Each change in mood has unseen yet deeply felt repercussions.

When she was little, Cathy would sometimes pretend to escape. She never got far, usually only a few yards down the road. Once she ran up and down the street with an open umbrella, hoping, like Mary Poppins, she'd get caught by a changing wind and be blown far away.

But the fact is, there isn't really anywhere to escape to.

Cathy can't escape her family. And I can't escape the man she calls her father, who comes to me and makes me do sexual things. It's my job to do what he says. When he looks at Cathy a certain way, or touches her on the back as he says goodnight, I know I have to be there when he comes to me later, let him do what he wants, and not make a noise.

Sometimes, when she is feeling particularly jittery, Cathy imagines that she is already dead. Dead, disembodied, and incredibly, incredibly relieved. From up in heaven (which in her imagination is about as high as a branch in a big old willow tree) she looks down at her grieving, horrified family, knowing that her hideous secret (whatever it is) is finally out. How sad they feel, how much they wish they had helped her! Oh why, they ask themselves, did this have to happen?

The way Cathy becomes disembodied varies. Usually she is run over by the school bus. Occasionally she is drowned in the local swimming pool after heroically trying to save a more popular classmate. Always she dies in a miraculously painless way. When I hear her thinking like this, I get mad. What Cathy doesn't realize is that, if she dies, there won't be any thinking. Not only that: if she dies, then I die, too. We can't ever fully escape from each other. Much as I'd like to deny it, we need each other. I know Cathy's secrets, and in return she feels some of my feelings. She gets to live in the everyday world, and I am jealous of that. But when she catches sight of me in the mirror, I know there's something I have that she wants, too.

Fragment Six: Are You Having a Happy Childhood?

WHEN CATHY WAS YOUNGER, her dad would sometimes ask her stupid questions, like did she enjoy adventures, did she really love him, and was she having a happy childhood.

Of course, she would always say yes. But she'd have a funny feeling in her stomach, something that told her her answer wasn't entirely true. The whole truth is complicated. Too complicated for either one of us to live with, so Cathy and I split it up. Sometimes, when I'm feeling really bad, I make Cathy cut herself with razor blades. I like to see the blood flow, to know I'm real. And sometimes, when she's feeling upset, Cathy writes poetry, and the words she writes are messages from me. They let her know she isn't totally crazy. If the poems reveal too many secrets, I scribble them out. Cathy and I work together that way. Like the letter Cathy's father once sent her, saying he cared about her, which he'd marked with an X and a note, "*Destroy after reading,*" everything Cathy and I do cancels itself out. We spend half our life trying to remember, the rest trying to forget. We spend half our time trying to tell, the rest trying to cover up the evidence. Because if someone found out our terrible secret, the vilest, most disgusting part of Cathy would be revealed.

So for now Cathy and I play the game. We give the people around us the answers they want, do what we're told, keep secrets, kiss when we have to, place our fingers in boiling water when we must, lie low, cover up the scars, and hide the real parts of ourselves. Most important, we keep writing poems.

Stark regiments of trees stand
Stripped naked
Against a sky of steel.
And the white bone of their souls
Seems taut in exposure
To this death unreal.
But deep in the earth at their feet
Seeds are held like secrets,
As snow falls,
And deep in the soul an unstirred germ endures
And softly calls.

Cathy believes that one day we'll get out of this place. We'll grow up and leave home, and things will change. She couldn't say how, but she knows this will be a good thing for her, even if the thought of it makes her feel sad and scared.

I, on the other hand, can't imagine any other kind of existence. I don't ever seem to feel older or to grow up. Perhaps because I know everything already. I've given up thinking it's not fair, or that someday someone will do something about it. I just get through each nighttime as best I can.

Fragment Seven: Repairing the Seam

BACK IN CATHY'S FORM ROOM, the bell goes. Lunchtime is over. Girls grab textbooks and head off to their next class. Cathy enjoys reading, enjoys studying, although she'd never admit it if anyone cool asked. English, French, history, and geography are her preferred subjects. But this afternoon she has double domestic science. Yuck!

Still, there's no getting around it. So she drags herself up the endless stairs and into the smelly, stuffy needlework classroom. She must be late. Some of the others are already seated at machines, threading them up like experts, passing black thread through mysterious brackets and holes.

Like most of her classmates, Cathy is working on a skirt. It's a stiff, grubby mass of corduroy, black and green with tiny pink flowers. Cathy feels as if she's been working on the skirt for half her life. Finally, today, she's joining the two big panels together, front and back. She's terrible at sewing, but there is something relaxing about the sound of sewing machines running, purring like cats as their claw-needles dance up and down. She fumbles her way around the one free Singer while Mrs. West, the needlework teacher, limps with her stiff leg between the heavily laden tables, inspecting her students' handiwork with a critical eye.

Separately, the two panels don't look like much. Together, though, they will make a whole skirt. Cathy can see that now. As she holds the two corduroy panels together, matching their edges up evenly, Cathy catches sight of her right thumb. There's a small scar on either side of the nail, a reminder of the day three winters ago when her thumb got caught in the hinge of a train door. Cathy and her mother had planned to go out for the day, but when Cathy peeled her mitten off after extricating her thumb, two deep, oozing cuts were revealed, so deep they had to be stitched up at the hospital. It was hard to believe the thumb would ever work again, but over the next few weeks the two sides knitted themselves back together and the stitches miraculously dissolved. A skirt ripped apart along a seam won't sew itself back together, but the two raw edges of a wound, even a bad one, will. If you tend them. So long as both edges are still there.

As Mrs. West despairs over someone else's jagged hemline, Cathy surreptitiously slides out a needle, a fine one, from the card of needles stored in the sewing machine. It's me who's making her do this, but she doesn't know that. She opens her right palm and pricks one of the fleshy pads underneath her fingers with the tip of the needle. It's only a small prick, barely deep enough to draw blood. A strange way to comfort yourself, perhaps, but it's something I needed. To feel a small pain, for an instant.

Fragment Eight: Together Apart

IT's ANOTHER LUNCHTIME, one week later, and the game is being played again. Despite Cathy's efforts to disappear, her classmates have decided not to let her off so easily this time. She reluctantly agrees to play, putting her book aside even though Frodo and Sam are within a day's march of the Crack of Doom. She can get back to it later, and it's important not to look like too much of a wimp.

"So what you have to do," says Kate, "is go into the rubbish bin, fish out that half-eaten biscuit that's covered in maggots, and finish it."

"Not likely!" says Cathy. Even someone as desperate as she is has limits. Anyway, that's the expected answer.

"Okay," says Kate. "Which do you choose, then: truth, dare, kiss, command, or promise?"

"Truth," I say, speaking, unnoticed, through Cathy.

"Okay," continues Kate, relishing the moment. All the other girls in the room have their eyes on Cathy. "Tell me, yes or no, are you a virgin?"

A laugh goes round Cathy's audience. Surely, in her case, the answer is yes.

"No," I say, before Cathy has a moment to think about it.

"Really?" says Kate. The question she would no doubt like to ask next is, "Who's the boy?" But the rule of the game is that she can only ask one question. So Cathy's safe for now.

Out in the world, Cathy feels strangely more whole. She doesn't know where this "untrue" answer came from, other than the hollowed-out place she knows she has inside. A place she's afraid to think about too much. Yet speaking from there has made her more solid, as if she has three dimensions instead of two.

Inside Cathy, I feel real. Less lonely, as though in that single instant when Kate looked at Cathy, she saw me as well.

"So," says Cathy, eager to change the subject. "Kate, you have to ask Debbie Birch to stamp on your foot." Debbie Birch is the biggest girl in the class, Kate one of the smallest.

"No, thanks!" says Kate.

"Which do you want, then?" asks Cathy, almost cheekily. While Kate deliberates, Cathy and I listen eagerly together, and for a minute, the two sides of our wound aren't so far apart.

The Damsite

Nan Germaine

WHEN I WAS SIXTEEN YEARS OLD I had secrets, all right. But my secrets were not exactly my own: they were the secrets of others. They were the confessions my mother made to me about her unhappiness. They were the actions of my father, which I observed when he took me with him on his business trips. I was the kind of girl people told secrets to; I took care to make myself one of those kinds of girls. I didn't tell anyone else my friends' secrets, at least not very often. My mother's and father's secrets I kept almost as well. But although they made me feel important at the time, they were burdens I carried long into adulthood.

I was the middle child, a girl with two brothers. My brothers were not really like boys. The older one was an owl-eyed intellectual who was the sole member of the history club in our small Montana town. The younger one was like a baby. That made me the only candidate to go with Dad when he inspected the hydroelectric dams around the state.

He liked to go on weekends. The mountain rivers were dammed only a couple of hours away from where we lived. These excursions would involve getting up at six on Saturday morning (another reason no one else in the family went: I was an early bird, and the early bird gets the secret). Dad and I would inspect one damsite, drive to another, stay over Saturday night in a small hotel near the company town, get up on Sunday and have a look around and maybe fish, or ski if it was winter, then drive back in time for dinner Sunday night.

I never thought it was odd to spend a weekend with my dad. I loved the big brick dam buildings, and the fabulous huge round pipes called penfolds that angled down from the high banks. I loved the huge signs that said DANGER, and KEEP OFF or KEEP OUT. I would pick my way along the riverbank and look for old junk, rusted smashed-up buckets, tin cans, uprooted and bleached trees with their great blossom of roots that had been torn up when the flow was heavy during spring runoff. What Dad himself inspected I never thought about.

I did not miss home or friends. I found it glamorous to be driving away in the car with my father, leaving Mom at home with the boys. I would doll up in black stretch pants that hooked under my heels and the green suede jacket with the fringe on which I had spent most of my after-school clerk's earnings. I had to wear a toque because it was always windy, but when I took it off I was careful to get quickly to the ladies' room. There I would brush the long blonde hair that, next to my trustworthy nature, was my best asset.

Once gone, however, I did worry about leaving my mom. I knew she was unhappy, and I was pretty sure she had no one to talk to but me. I mean, who would be drawn to open her heart to a furrow-browed, acne-chinned introvert like my brother Daniel? And Byron could barely sit still long enough to eat a sandwich. My mom did have friends, but her problems were not the sort she could tell a friend. Her friends all seemed happily married, and they would not understand at all.

Whereas I did. I understood a lot, and I was a good listener; I seemed to have wisdom far beyond my age. That's what people said. It always surprised me that others hadn't noticed when, for instance, two of my friends competed to impress a new guy, or when one of the popular kids was getting edged out of the clique. At slumber parties girls tended to cry on my shoulder and ask me what to do about their boyfriends. This was flattering and I encouraged it.

I am not certain I had encouraged my mother's confidences, however. I think they just came to me because she had no one else. I did like to help her cook. Food naturally inspired both of us to talk. We baked together for most holidays, although we didn't talk much while we did, except about the dough or the icing sugar. Where we talked was in the supermarket, and at the greengrocer's, and in the car coming and going. We window-shopped for food the way other people did for clothes.

That corn looks okay; not great, though. Let's go over and see if the IGA has some.

They do, but it's way more expensive.

Doesn't look as fat, either. But look at that—Rainier cherries...

I knew where to find fresh chicken livers for pâté and how to browbeat the fishmonger to make sure what was called fresh hadn't already been frozen and thawed. To tell the truth I was better at shopping than at cooking, and so was my mother. She wasn't enough of a hedonist to really love food; she made herself into a good cook by rote, both because she hated to do things badly and because she wanted so much to please my dad. I was different; I truly loved the taste of lemon curd or smoked trout, the stuff we bought from the Natives who came in the truck.

It must have been on one of these shopping trips out of the house that my mother began to tell me her problems. They were mostly, in fact they were all, to do with my dad.

He just gets so angry. I don't know how to handle it, she'd say.

My father did go into sulks where he didn't speak for days. I knew he was punishing her, or us.

He thinks there's only one way to do things; that was another thing she said.

I can't tell your father—

He'll be angry—

He's been angry since last week. It doesn't help that he was drinking Scotch—

On and on it went. I don't remember the specifics. I

don't want to. I guess I must have wanted to hear it, then. He was a difficult man, temperamental, and determined to have his way. There were no beatings. There was no drug abuse. There was too much drinking, but that was the same as with everyone else we knew, and it didn't seem to slow him down.

Our trips down the coffee and tea aisle of the supermarket would become agonizingly slow, and finally stop, as my mother stood with one wrist draped across her eyebrows, hiding or half-hiding the fear and pain in her eyes.

Last night he—she'd begin.

And like the good listener and good friend I was, I stood there. I loaned her my anger and even my outrage.

Oh, that's awful...Why can't he see that...You shouldn't have to put up with...Well, if it's like that why don't you just tell him off?

Oh, I couldn't.

Why don't you just say—

Oh, you don't understand. You know what he'd do—

The weak spot in my system of good listening was that I ended every session with a goad to action. It never worked with my girlfriends, either. I don't know why I thought it would work with my mother. But I wanted to stop the litany. I wanted to stop her pain. Because no matter how unintentionally comic it appeared, confessions whispered in the canned goods section of the supermarket, it was not funny. I knew that. My mother's desperation was real. Her suffering was real. I wanted it to end.

With all the wisdom of my sixteen years I counseled

her. Be brave and stand up to him, I said. Tell him to snap out of his "moods."

Her mouth hung down at either end.

I can't, she'd say.

Finally I found myself counseling her to leave, because it all sounded so hopeless. Just leave. Get a divorce. Terrible, shocking word in the early sixties.

Oh, I couldn't, she'd say. What would I do?

You do have a teaching degree, I'd remind her.

But apparently that wouldn't help.

I can't, she'd say, defeated by both him and me.

I didn't understand "can't." All I knew is that the story of her unhappiness led, time and again, to this slammed, thick, oak-beamed, iron-strapped, padlocked door: She. Could. Not. Do anything about her unhappiness, that is. And it always led to this: I. Must. Not. Tell. My dad.

Which of course I wouldn't. How could I tell him, and what?

So we would buy the sultanas and the nutmeg for the rice pudding, and by the time we got back to the house my mother's face would have rearranged itself into another, happier one. The ends of her mouth would work themselves around, sometimes even turning up a little, which was surely what she intended them to do. That was the face the others saw. I was the privileged child, the one who had seen her real face. Or so it felt, then. We would bake the rice pudding, sticking our fingers into the mixture and sucking on them. But at dinnertime when we were all together, I noticed that neither my mother nor I had much to eat.

That was why I worried about leaving my mother when I went off to look at the hydroelectric dams with my father.

But the attractions of those outings far outweighed the inconveniences. Driving in the closed car into the rising foothills, the winter sun behind us, felt daring. Dad did not talk much and neither did I. That was what it was like with men, I figured, and I enjoyed it. I did not have to sympathize, because he did not complain, and I did not have to lend strength, because he seemed to have plenty of his own. He wasn't moody or difficult, either, when we were on our trips. That made me a little smug. So Mom couldn't handle him, eh? I could; it was easy.

Often we'd stop for gas and sometimes we'd even pick up a hitchhiker. Our first site was usually the Horseshoe Falls Dam near the little town of Wallace on the Silver River. There were two buildings there, the first one built in 1918 and the second one in the 1930s, to supply Billings with electric power. There were a couple of Bailey bridges over the canyon that the river had carved through the foothills country, and that was where I headed. I was quite happy on my own for the hours Dad took doing whatever it was he did. Sometimes I'd look back from the brow of the hill, or up from low ground beside the turquoise flowing water, and I'd see him, with a clipboard in his hand, edging his way out along some sort of walkway over the reservoir. He'd be busy but he'd wave at me.

For lunch, there was the lunchroom with two or three tables with plastic cloths over them set out in the yard behind the general store. The store was neat and bright and had all kinds of old things you couldn't get anywhere else, as well as ice cream and fishing lures and walking sticks. We'd have a bologna sandwich (I never was allowed to eat one at home) and then most likely we'd only have an hour or so before we moved on.

How is it, Dad?

Oh, it's pretty good, pretty good. They keep it in pretty good shape here.

Are we going to go to the Timberline?

That was my favorite hotel. I thought it was glamorous, because the dining room was shaped like a horseshoe and you could see mountain sheep grazing out in front of the picture windows.

By two in the afternoon we were heading back to the car, and by 3:30 or 4:00 we'd be checking in to the hotel. We might call home then, to see how Mom was. We'd go for a walk to see if the sheep were nearby, or the bears, and before too long we'd be thinking about dinner.

At this time of day, I did sometimes find my father a little difficult to handle. He would start to get fidgety. Then he'd mention that he had to get something from the liquor store. There was no liquor store near the hotel; you had to go in to town, about a half-hour drive, to get to it, so I never wanted him to go. I had no luck talking him out of it, though. Saturday afternoons found me meekly curled up on a sofa in the hotel lounge reading my book while Dad went out to get some Scotch. This wobbled my confidence a little, but I tried to stay well wrapped up in my book and the time passed quickly. He'd return, striding across the hotel lobby under the big stag horns. We'd go back up to the room, where he poured himself a Scotch. And then we'd start to think about dinner again.

We usually ate beef: that's what people did. I wasn't usually hungry enough. After dinner, another problem: Dad would be snoozy and want to watch a little television and then fall asleep. Or he'd chat to some man at another table. He might strike up a conversation with the manager of the hotel. They got to know my dad, these people, because he did this trip every couple of months. Once he even got involved in a long conversation with the hitch-hiker we'd picked up earlier. I was pretty insulted by that. I would not be sleepy and I wanted to play games—Monopoly, or checkers. My grandfather would play those games with me, even my idiotic older brother would, but not my Dad.

We always shared a hotel room; there wasn't enough money for two, and no one ever thought twice about it. I would get into one single bed and he would be heading for the other single bed and most times he would get into it and we'd say goodnight and go to sleep.

Those times I remember as being good.

But I know it wasn't always that way and that sometimes he'd leave his pajamas untouched and he would go out of the room. I know it made me feel uneasy when he left, but I didn't know what he did in the hotel.

ON ONE OF THESE TRIPS, however, I found out. We had done our usual visit to the Horseshoe Dam. I'd picked raspberries by the road cuts and had a fine old time. The lady at the general store gave us beef barley soup and grilled cheese sandwiches for lunch. She was new. And we got to the Timberline on time. We were waiting at the check-in desk for Dad to sign something when it happened.

He looked up and saw a woman crossing the lobby. The woman smiled at us and waved. He waved back.

Well, look who's here, he said.

It was very *very* phony. I knew it was a setup.

Who's that? I said. She was still on the other side of the big open space.

Oh, it's Mrs. Devine.

That was no one I knew.

Don't you remember Mrs. Devine, from the office?

Vaguely, I decided, I knew the name. She wasn't my dad's secretary, but she was someone else's secretary in the company. Once a year my parents had a big party and everyone came over to the house and stood around in the garden swatting mosquitoes and drinking cocktails and eating little sausage rolls that Mom burned her fingers on, pulling out of the oven.

Maybe. I could just recall one of my mother's monologues about the people at the party: And there's Mrs. Devine, she's divorced and she has two boys. One of them is always in trouble...

What's *she* doing here? I asked.

I don't know, said Dad, with a jolly air about him, a far too jolly air, but we can find out.

Right then I knew he was lying. He was a better liar

than some, but not good enough to get this one by his only daughter. And strangely, I became like my mother. I could not say to him, You're lying. You do know what she's doing here and you're not one bit surprised to see her. So I said nothing, and he scampered off after her. She ended up joining us for dinner, which was torture. She was a little bit coarse, or she had bad skin; her face was thicker than my mother's and she was not at all sexy, I thought. But I suffered through dinner because I knew when it was over, we'd all stand up and push our chairs in and we'd say good-night and that would be the end of it. I was pretty sure that Mrs. Devine was here by arrangement, but I had no thought at all that this arrangement would extend beyond dinner.

But it did not happen quite that way. First of all, between courses, I said I had to go to the washroom. And I had some kind of problem with my clothing. There was a rip in my black stretch pants or a button off my blouse. Dad had noticed it. He always noticed things like that. It could really put you off your stride. Anyway, he noticed this and he said maybe I should go to the washroom to fix it and that maybe Mrs. Devine could come in and help me. She had a safety pin.

This I did not like.

I ended up in one of those small rooms and I was squished in front of the sink in that garish white light in front of a mirror with the curious and snoopy Mrs. Devine. She kind of stared at me and admired my hair, which did look pretty good that day. She didn't want to get right down to the business of my clothing, but she wanted to talk. She said something about my driving test that was coming up, and had I got any better at parallel parking? This told me that she had prior knowledge of me and I did not think it had come from the secretarial pool at the office. When I mumbled my shocked response she still looked at me. She didn't say much but she was taking pleasure, I think, in getting to know a little bit about me. It was a creepy feeling. I felt for the first time in all this as if I were betraying my mother. I could tell that Mrs. Devine was curious about me and her curiosity was because she was close to my father, not because I was some kind of superior sixteen-year-old that she had a yearning to know.

It was an affront in so many ways I could not even sort them out. I was frosty as she attached this safety pin to whatever part of my outfit had come adrift. Seriously frosty. And she got it. She went from being near a confession herself (God save me, as my mother would say) to poking herself in the finger and backing off.

Dad was sitting at the table when we came out. He had a half-expectant look but quickly adjusted it when he saw how huffy I was. What on earth was the man up to? To this day I ask myself: What could possibly have been going through his mind?

Did he have to see his mistress that day? Did she have to come to the Timberline Hotel, and meet me, and eye me in the mirror like a speculative buyer looking at a used car: Can I handle this girl if I should inherit her? Did he talk to her about leaving my mother?

I never asked him.

After dinner we said goodnight to Mrs. Devine. Dad and I went back to the hotel room together. I was tired and got into my bed. He was twitchy, and he did not get into his bed. He started looking through his suitcase and he discovered that he did not have his flask. That meant, he explained to me, that he would have to go out to the liquor store. Now I am pretty sure that at nine p.m. on a Saturday night in Montana in 1966 there was no liquor store open. However, I said sure, Dad, and turned my back to him. And he said he would not be long.

But he was long.

My father was gone for at least an hour, maybe two. It was a very long time for me, lying in that bed, waiting for him to open the door and come back in, brightly, as he always did, his mood improved, as it always was. And as the time stretched on I suffered. I did not—I return to my innocent self here, because although I knew everyone's secrets I actually didn't know much about anything and certainly not about people's fathers having affairs; that was right outside of my experience—actually *suspect* that he had gone to this woman's bed. I couldn't do that.

I just waited for him to come back, and as he did not come back I struggled between my knowledge and my innocence, between what I could not fail to observe and what I refused to acknowledge. My body would not be still. I was full of tension, like a buzzing electric wire. My shoulders were hard as boards and I wanted to cry. I was scared in that room, by myself, and I felt abandoned. I missed my mother and I needed to talk to someone. But

I could not telephone her because I could not tell. And I couldn't cry because he might come in at any minute.

I left the bedside lamp on, on his side. When he came in I pretended I was asleep. He didn't say anything; he climbed into his bed. The night passed, the morning came. Mrs. Devine was not at breakfast. I did not mention her. Dad did not mention her. We went to the next damsite. I wasn't having any fun. Clouds covered the sun. I didn't like the junk along the river. We set off for home. It was quiet in the car, but a different quiet. Intentional. When we were having dinner Mom asked brightly how the trip had gone.

It was fine, I said.

Did you get to the Timberline? she said.

Yes, I said. And you know what? Mrs. Devine was there.

I had not made a decision to tell his secret. I just did it. I wanted my mom to know. Her eyes fled to my father's, and he jerked a little bit as if he'd touched one of those wires and I thought, well, let them work it out. I guess I didn't want the secrets any more.

Unseen, Unheard

Kelys Green

I STILL HAVE THE SCAR under my left breast that I got
when I was eleven years old. I hadn't cleaned my room. I
hated cleaning my room. My mother had come home tired
from work, seen the mess, and said quietly that I would
get it when she told my father. That was her solution to
her own anger. When she was upset with me, she'd say,
"Just wait until your father gets here. I'm too tender-hearted
to deal with you." I didn't think too much of my mother's
kind heart.

Nothing was more terrifying than my father in a rage,
and rage seemed to be one of the things he did best. I
spent the whole evening with my gut cramping in dread
of my father's arrival. When he showed up, he was drunk.
He often was. My mother told him about the awful, defi-
ant thing I'd done. He started shouting at me. The thing
that made him most angry was a disobedient child. He

grabbed up a wooden hanger from somewhere; the floor, maybe. I started running. As I ran, I looked over my shoulder at the ravening ogre lumbering after me. I didn't see the doorknob until I crashed right into it, just below my left nipple. I was in early puberty, and my budding breasts ached all the time. When my chest rammed into the doorknob, I went nearly unconscious from the agony. My knees buckled. That's why my father caught me. He didn't notice I was injured, that I was having trouble standing. He beat me until the hanger broke.

What was the big secret in my world? *I* was. Anything I was thinking or feeling, I kept to myself. You could say I was only being an obedient child. "Children should be seen and not heard," my Jamaican father would tell me. And if I tried to explain my side of the story when he'd mistakenly accused me of something, he'd forbid me to speak. "Don't defend yourself," he'd hiss. "Don't defend yourself." He beat me whenever he could convince himself that I deserved it, which was often. Sometimes I didn't even understand what it was I had done wrong.

I thought my parents hated me, so I tried to make myself invisible. I tried to do what I was told. I kept my mouth shut. I didn't let them know when I was angry or sad. I certainly didn't let them know when I was happy; that didn't happen much, anyway. I didn't tell them about my nightmares. I didn't tell them that the friend they'd asked to babysit me had been fondling me and sticking his tongue in my mouth.

The weird thing was, there was plenty of good about

my parents. My mother was the best cook in the world. She could make anything taste marvelous. (Except tripe.) She laughed when I ate bony chicken with my hands, because she liked to do that too, even though it made my father grimace at our bad manners. She liked to dance. She taught me how. She taught me how to cook all my favorite foods, and how to sew. My father could sing, and when I was really little, he let me waltz with him by standing on his feet. Whenever he'd been away, he always brought me back a present, even though I knew he didn't have a lot of money to spend. My parents knew that I loved to read, and they let me read anything I could get my hands on. And if I was sick or hurt—except that time with the wooden hanger—they were both the gentlest, most caring nurses. Years later, I would come to understand that my parents had loved me the best way they knew how. They had raised me the way their parents raised them. They were trying to make me into a good person. But when I was young, I was convinced they wanted to kill me. That they were only waiting for an excuse to do so.

My mother was from Barbados. I was born there, too. In the Caribbean, many believe that you must beat children into submission or they'll never become decent people. Not everyone does it, but it's pretty commonplace. I guess it makes sense, coming as we do from a history of slavery. During those times, if you were allowed to keep your children, you knew that you'd better train them to obedience fast, before massa did it for you; his whip flayed skin off backs. Compared to that, the whack of an open hand on a backside probably seemed like a piece of cake. It might even save your children's lives.

When I was sixteen, my parents moved to Canada. They found a house to rent in Etobicoke, a suburban part of Toronto. I stayed on in Barbados with my grandmother to finish my Ordinary Level exams, then joined my parents a few months later. By then I had become so good at keeping the secret of me that even *I* didn't know who I was. I tried not to think about things that made me uncomfortable. Sometimes I didn't know what I felt.

I arrived in Canada on a hot day in the middle of the season people called summer. Where I had come from, we had two rainy seasons and a dry season. My parents took me to our new home, something called a "townhouse" in the middle of a new housing division. The house was joined to all the houses around it. That seemed weird to me. Our house had four stories instead of spreading out all on one floor, like the houses I'd been used to. One of the levels in our new home was an underground basement—that was unfamiliar to me, too. The basement was dark and felt chilly to someone used to dry tropical air. The windows of the house were covered with heavy drapes and blinds that it would take me years to learn how to open and close. Being inside was like being sealed in a coffin.

That first day, we didn't spend a lot of time indoors. My parents took me out to their new backyard, gave me a meal. The backyard was a small square of perfectly manicured grass. I would soon come to miss the sprawling, lawn-free backyards I had known (who knew that you could miss hard-packed dirt?), shaded by the occasional mango or breadfruit tree. I would come to miss the huge patch of yellow chrysanthemums that had resulted when a pot of mums spilled in our garden in Barbados and spread. I would remember the spicy scent of them when I discovered that chrysanthemums in Canada had no scent at all. I would come to miss having flowers year-round. I would miss trees that bore fruit; I would miss watermelon slices that didn't taste of plastic from being wrapped in Cling Wrap.

But that first day, I sat with my family in the green, barren little backyard and we caught up with each other. I don't remember what I told them. I didn't think about it much. Eventually, my father said with a knowing smile, "Guess what time it is."

The sun was still high in the sky, warm on my skin. "About four o'clock?" I replied.

My parents laughed. It was nearly nine p.m. In the Caribbean, sitting right on the equator, sunset is at about six p.m. every day, year-round. I squinted up at the sun and tried to understand that I had come to a place where daylight extended far into the night, at least part of the year.

Etobicoke in the seventies was an odd place to a Caribbean teenager. The racial makeup of the people around me would become more varied in the decades that followed, but then it seemed as though everyone was white. I missed the rainbow of skin colors and races that make up the tropics. My new neighbors spoke with an accent that sounded deadpan to the ears of someone used to the cadences of Caribbean speech. I would eventually learn to hear and appreciate the nuances of a Toronto accent, but I couldn't in the beginning. And white people looked at us funny, my parents and me. The kind of expression you might get if you turned a corner and bumped into a large dog: apprehension, then exaggerated relief when the dog wags its tail. We heard terrifying stories: of white people pushing black people into the paths of oncoming subway trains; of white schoolchildren ganging up on individual black or South Asian ones.

White people, even the friendly ones, asked me why I didn't go back to the tropics where it was warm. It was as though they wanted to keep their country—where they could have new cars and lakeside cottages—all for themselves. A white man tried to bar me from entering an apartment building where I had been invited to dinner at my teacher's house. He demanded to know what I was doing there. When I told him, he replied, "Huh. Never can tell with you people," and grudgingly let me pass. I once got on a bus too slowly to suit the bus driver, and he pressed his hand to my back and shoved me farther down the aisle. (I didn't think he'd done anything wrong at the time; I knew that adults could do whatever they wanted to children.) Even though there were plenty of friendly white people, there were still these disturbing incidents of hatred of us with our dark skins. You can act as nicely as you please, but you can't hide your skin. I can see now why my parents might be so fearful for my safety that they would want to discipline me into unquestioning obedience. The world can be a dangerous place for black people.

But my parents weren't going to get support in their new country for controlling their offspring. I remember clearly something my mother said to me in those first few months. I don't recall what I'd done this time to make her angry, but she told me, "You aren't even allowed to discipline your children in this place. If you beat them, the children can call the police on you." I could? Despite how odd I found everything, I began to think that maybe I'd come to heaven.

My parents had enrolled me in high school. My Caribbean education put me ahead a year, so now I was a sixteen-year-old in a class with eighteen- and nineteen-year-olds. As if that wasn't daunting enough, some of them were boys! I had always gone to gender-segregated schools. I found the boys loud and physically intimidating. I couldn't meet their eyes. At least school itself was familiar, an ugly, blocky building like schools everywhere, with some teachers you liked and some you didn't.

I was good at English and French, and I liked my English teacher, who was my homeroom teacher. I liked my history teacher, too, because he made history into stories and got me interested. It was easier to remember the names and the dates when I was fascinated by the story. I especially liked my biology teacher, Mr. Maeshima. Like me, he seemed to think biology was fun. He smiled and made jokes all through class. He enjoyed dissecting animals as much as I did, and he didn't look embarrassed the day someone asked what a sex change was, and I stood up and explained to the class how surgeons could turn a penis inside out and tuck it inside the person's body to make a vagina. (All the reading I did had taught me things many of my schoolmates didn't know.)

Slowly I did the work of learning to navigate my new school. I tried to figure out what was fashionable to wear. My parents couldn't buy me lots of clothes, but I had a sewing machine, and I could sometimes afford fabric and patterns with my allowance. I never got the styles quite right, though, and I could see the judgment on the faces of my female classmates. I learned how to understand North American humor, but I never did learn how to socialize very well. I think it was a little too late for that. What with looking odd, sounding odd, acting odd, and showing up in the final year of high school, when the other students had formed friendships and clique groups going back years, there was no way I could have fit in. On weekends I stayed at home, did my chores, and read. Whenever I was bored or sad or lonely, there was always reading.

After holiday weekends, some of my white school-mates, the well-off ones, would ask me if I had "gone to the cottage." I'd shake my head no. I tried explaining that we didn't have a cottage, that we couldn't have afforded one anyway, but they didn't understand. People stopped trying to talk to me. I brought no friends home because I had no friends. In some ways, that was easier. My dad had stopped beating me when I was in my mid-teens, but he never talked about it, so I never knew if he would start up again. I still lived in terror of his rages. The less of a social life I had, the less suspicious and threatening my parents were.

Then, at age seventeen, I started university. There I was a stranger among strangers, so I wasn't as ostracized. I attended frosh orientation events, at least those that I could get home from before my curfew. I discovered that the word "Triumph" on the T-shirt I was so fond of wearing was the name of a rock band, not an expression of what I wanted to do in life. In a few months I reached the legal drinking age of eighteen. I learned to like beer. I still didn't have close friends, but now I had a group of friendly, familiar people with whom to hang out. In my first and second year they were all white, but I began to learn the differences between Italian and Irish and Ukrainian. I taught them about Caribbean rum cake. We learned about each other.

I finally had people who invited me to spend time with them—which meant that I had a big problem. Although I was eighteen, legally an adult, my parents were still scrutinizing everything I did. They didn't want me turning up pregnant. But slowly, reluctantly, they began allowing me more and more freedom, and slowly, hesitantly, I tried it on for size.

One February night I stayed out drinking with my newfound friends until the bars closed. It was well past my curfew. I got a lift to our housing division, but I had my friends stop the car on the street outside it. I didn't want the headlights or the sound of the car alerting my parents that I was late. I tiptoed up to our front door. The living room was in darkness. I looked up to my parents' second-floor bedroom window. The lights were out. Sometimes my parents fell asleep before I got home. I prayed that this was one of those times. Maybe I could sneak in without them knowing.

I was a little drunk. I fumbled around in my purse for my key, but couldn't find it. I felt in my pockets. No key there. Had I taken it with me that morning? I couldn't remember. It was cold standing on the doorstep. The familiar cramps of fear started in my stomach as I thought about ringing the doorbell.

Then I remembered another secret I had. I had discovered that the living room window on the main floor at the back of the house was faulty; its lock didn't work. I hadn't told my parents, because it no longer occurred to me to tell them anything. Hope made my stomach churn even more. Maybe I wouldn't have to face my father's wrath!

A bit dizzy from the alcohol, I walked down our little street and round to the back of the string of townhouses. I crunched through knee-high snow, along the pathways between our backyards. Melting snow trickled down into my boots. I started to shiver. I made it through our back gate. Woozily, I got to the window that led into the living room. My teeth were clacking together in the freezing winter night. Two years in Canada, and I still wasn't used to winter. With the heel of my mittened hand, I jammed at the window, trying desperately not to make any noise. I just wanted to be inside where it was warm. I just wanted not to get caught.

The window slid open. I was so happy. I pushed it open

a little more, wriggled through, and stood up in our living room.

Sure, I was slightly drunk, but why did everything look so different? Oh. My mother must have rearranged the furniture again. She was always doing that. Then I realized that the furniture was a different color than it had been that morning. And now there was a thick white carpet on the floor. I tried to make my sodden mind work. Could my parents have bought new furniture and this expensive carpet and had them installed during the day?

Then I realized that I was not in my own home, but in the neighbors'. I had broken into our neighbors' house at two a.m. and was standing dripping water onto their carpet. And I was a black woman, and they were very white.

Now, that last thought wasn't particularly reasonable. If the neighbors had come downstairs to discover *anyone* breaking into their house, I'm sure they'd have been just as scared, whether the interloper was white, black, or green with pink polka dots. But I lived in a world in which my skin color put me in danger. How much more so when I had in fact done something wrong?

I went even colder than I had been standing out in the backyard. I had never seen a rifle, except on television, but I suddenly had an image of the neighbor turning one on me. I don't remember getting back out that window, but I do remember knowing that at all cost I must do it *quietly*. People say that if something threatening happens to you when you're drunk, you sober up immediately. That's a crock. My brain was still processing thoughts at the speed of maple syrup in winter. I kept trying to think smarter, faster, but it wasn't working. I don't remember walking out of the neighbors' backyard and into the one I hoped was my own. I do remember looking very carefully through this new back window, enumerating each piece of furniture until I was certain it was my home.

Same procedure. I got in safely. My parents still weren't awake. I looked down at the water dripping off my boots. I'd been walking through virgin snow, so I hadn't tracked in any mud. The water would dry overnight, and there'd be no telltale signs on my parents' floor, or on the neighbors'.

I crept upstairs. I went to bed. I kept my secret.

Cherry Pride

Susan Musgrave

IN THE TOWN WHERE I GREW UP, we used to hang out at a beach called Cherry Pride. At low tide, the beach smelled like rotten eggs because our town dumped its raw sewage into the sea. Whenever something happened that was supposed to be hushed up (an abortion, an extramarital affair), people would say, "Smells a lot like Cherry Pride." In other words, a dirty little secret was causing a great big stink.

Cherry Pride ran under a bridge, and it was the one place we could go to make out or smoke up without anyone—the cops, our parents—bugging us. We went to a lot of trouble to make it our own. One summer a kid who had moved to our school from Germany volunteered to do community work, and he picked up more than a dozen condoms on that small strip of beach his first afternoon.

My best friend, Delphine, and I used to go there to

write poetry. We smoked, too, but not cigarettes. Delphine said she'd never speak to me again if I took up smoking tobacco. "You'll end up getting that cancer," she said. Neither of us had made the cheerleading team (I had crooked teeth and Delphine had been on crutches ever since her car accident), so we hunkered down under the bridge, dedicating odes to (among our other role models) Count Dracula.

Not long after the accident in which her boyfriend and another kid from our class were killed, Delphine confided in me that she wished she had died on the highway, too. She didn't want to live any more, she said, and she planned to do something about it. But, she added, she didn't want to take the easy way out—whatever that meant.

Del made me promise not to tell anyone, especially her mother, because she figured her mother would interfere and try to stop her.

"What am I supposed to do," I said, "sit on my butt and let you put your head in the microwave? What sort of best friend would let a friend do that?" But she said, "I'd do the same for you, if you were the one who was hurting."

When she put it like that, I had to respect her wishes. But I was worried, *and* angry, and I decided I'd keep her under surveillance. If it looked like she was even *thinking* about taking herself out, I was going to call her mother, even if it meant Del didn't trust me after that. At least she'd be alive to hate me, and one day she'd maybe look back and thank me.

The cops had found an ounce of pot in Delphine's

backpack at the scene of the car accident. We all got the afternoon off school to attend the funeral of her boyfriend and the other kid, but the next morning the principal called us down to the gymnasium for an assembly. Every time something major happened, the cops came out in force to our school and we had an assembly. As soon as they had us all sitting in straight rows on the gymnasium floor, they would try to convince us we had a duty to tell on anyone who sold or used drugs.

I had read about a girl in California who informed on her liberal parents for smoking pot. She'd been brainwashed about drugs in a high school guidance course. Her parents got sentenced to jail time, and she was put in care. In a foster home. The judge said that her parents were not fit for the responsibility of raising her, and that this girl would be better off in a God-fearing home. I figured that meant the kind where they made you take baths in ice cubes if you lipped off, or tied your hands to the bedposts at night to keep you from bad touching. That girl really blew it, and I felt sorry for her. It was worse for the parents, though. Being liberals, they must have asked themselves a thousand times, "Where did we go wrong?"

Delphine was still in the hospital from the accident, with her wrecked leg in a cast, up in the air. The cops told us that if we maintained our "code of silence" and chose not to speak up about who had supplied her with drugs, we should ask ourselves exactly what sort of individuals we thought we were protecting. If we knew their names, didn't we have a moral obligation to come forward and give the police the information they needed to make an arrest? Not likely. *Nobody talks, everybody walks,* that was our motto.

I remembered the time the cops had brought a sniffing dog to our school, and Delphine started freaking out because we'd stashed all the dope we had for sale that week in her locker. She figured the dog was going to finger her, but he didn't. Del thought she'd got lucky because the dog had a cold that day. We both had a good laugh about it, anyway.

Having to keep Delphine's secret, that she might try to commit suicide, weighed me down, became a burden on me. For a while I tried keeping a diary, a safe place, I believed, where I could unload my secrets. But then I started worrying that my brother would pick the lock. He couldn't bear not knowing every deranged thing that went on inside my head, I knew, as if he thought knowing would make it easier for him to make my life hell. So I kept Delphine's secret to myself. Pretty much everything in my life was a secret in those days, from someone or other. Only I didn't think of it that way. I thought of it as just the way it was.

I hadn't always been so discreet. In kindergarten, the girl next to me tickled me at naptime and made me giggle, meaning I got sent out into the hall. When I told on her, I got to go back to my nap-mat, and the girl was put in the hall in my place. After that, most of the kids wouldn't lay their mats down next to mine. The lesson? Even when something wasn't fair, you kept your mouth shut. You took your lumps.

But I was a slow learner. In grade four, Mrs. Hemmion called me into the cloakroom one afternoon and told me she had to be out of the class for an hour. She appointed me class monitor and asked me to report anyone who acted up. I ratted out every one of my classmates. "Max was laughing and telling jokes. Ian threw spitballs," I told Mrs. Hemmion. "Denise was looking through the papers on your desk. Lynn erased our homework from the blackboard." Mrs. Hemmion seemed pleased with my undercover work, but when I went home and bragged to my parents they went to the principal and said they would not have their daughter used as some kind of Nazi informer. Up until that point they had never criticized anything about school, so I knew this had to be serious.

I made up my mind, right then and there, never to tell on anyone, no matter how bad or illegal a thing they'd done. Not even when X tried to burn down our school in the middle of the night the week before final exams in grade nine, and we all had to switch to a school two bus zones away because our school was smoke-damaged and the whole place had to be cordoned off by the police. Not even when I heard on the radio that some anonymous person had offered a $10,000 reward for information leading to the arrest of whoever had set the fire. I was secretly glad that at last something really criminal and worthwhile had happened in our town; most of us hated that school and wished it had burned to the ground. Del said we could have bought a lot of drugs with the $10,000, but I told her I wouldn't have enjoyed getting high knowing that X was in prison or, worse, the local psychiatric bin.

I felt sorry for X. When he was a kid, he'd put the live

end of an electrical cord in his mouth (the other end was plugged into the wall) and his mouth ended up halfway across his face. Everyone picked on him, naturally. Rubber Mouth, Tumor Face, Evil Satan Ferret. Those were just a few of the names we called him. We were brutal, I'll admit it. Delphine thought it was the reason X tried to burn down the school, to get some of his self-esteem back. You couldn't blame him, I guess.

I felt especially bad about keeping Delphine's secret from my boyfriend, Billy. Billy didn't believe in secrets. He shot from the hip and he was usually right on target. That was one of the things I liked best about him.

My parents didn't like Billy; my father thought he "wasn't good enough" for me. *Water seeks its own level:* that's how he put it. My parents thought I should be dating boys I had "something in common with." In other words, white boys who came from our neighborhood, not Billy, who was Native and lived on the reserve.

Billy didn't have a car, except for his dad's rusted-out Toyota (no windows, all four tires sold for parts), where we sometimes went when we wanted to be alone. We'd sit in his driveway pretending we had someplace to go, anywhere, really, as long as it was away. Billy wanted me to have his baby; I guess he thought he could hold on to me that way. I didn't have the heart to tell him I didn't plan on having kids, not ever—I figured there were already enough unwanted children in the world. So I had to keep it a secret from him that I was using protection. Every month, when my period came, I would act all disappointed.

Even though I didn't want to get pregnant, I was in love with Billy—something else I didn't tell anyone.

Before Billy, I had another boyfriend, the kind my parents approved of. Ritchie called my father "sir" and complimented my mother on her Nanaimo bars. He played a lot of sports at school, was captain of the football team. Up until I started going out with him, my parents had always warned me not to get attached to any one boy. I should "play the field," they said, as if dating was some kind of a game. With Ritchie, it turned into a blood sport.

Ritchie took my virginity one hot day down at Cherry Pride, in an abandoned boathouse. First he lit a banana slug on fire; I watched it melt into a pool of sticky ooze. Then he undid his zipper, pulled out his penis, and said, "Put your mouth on it." I did, worrying that I'd cut him with my crooked teeth. When nothing happened, he forced me down on the boathouse floor and wedged his knee between my legs.

I was crying by this time and pleading with Ritchie to stop. He didn't stop. He said if I didn't shut up he would do something to me so that I'd never be able to open my mouth again. I was afraid that he was going to drown me and my body would be found washed up with the seaweed and the garbage on the beach at Cherry Pride. I promised, if he let me go, I wouldn't tell anyone what he'd done. I would keep it a secret. I wouldn't tell my parents, or Delphine, or even Mrs. Bellis, our school guidance counselor. When he did let me go, I was *so* grateful to be alive. I walked home and ran a hot bath. I lay there, soaking, until the water got cold.

THE SUMMER AFTER I GOT TOGETHER WITH BILLY, my parents decided we should spend more time together as a family. Stuck at the wilderness cottage they rented, I pined for my life. I resented the leech-infested lake, the outhouse with its "If you sprinkle when you tinkle, be a sweetie and wipe the seatie" sign, the fact that Billy was more than five hundred miles away down south. When I got back to town after a month of peeling the scabs off my mosquito bites and picking mouse droppings out of the butter, I found out that Delphine had slashed her wrists.

I went to visit her in the hospital. Her skin looked pale and she kept falling asleep on me—I had to shake her awake. She said she'd waited until I was out of town, because she knew I would have tried to talk her out of it. But instead of bleeding to death the way she'd envisioned it, something totally unexpected had happened to her, she told me drowsily. She'd found a friend in Jesus. He'd appeared before her that night under the bridge, right as she started losing consciousness, and shone his Light in her eyes. I didn't have the heart to tell her it had probably been a cop shining his cop-flashlight in her face to see if he should radio for a body bag or just a stretcher.

I felt excluded. It was Jesus, not me, who'd been there for Delphine. He hadn't done all that great a job, that's what I thought, but Delphine had been Born Again, and I could see there was nothing I could do that was going to change it. She said Jesus was going to heal all her wounds, both inside and out, because she had faith, she believed in Him. She made me promise I wouldn't say a word to anyone.

She was afraid it would get back to her parents. After all she'd put them through, she said, she didn't want to upset them any further. She worried her father would start drinking again. Her mother was open-minded; she'd think she was a total failure if she found out her only daughter had become a Christian.

Before I left, I asked Delphine how she was going to keep Jesus a secret from her parents. She said she would pray in private, under the covers at night, with a flashlight. I didn't see why you'd need a flashlight to pray, but that must have been because I didn't have a personal relationship, the way she had, with the Lord.

"Your secret is safe with me," I told her. Delphine seemed to be sliding in and out of sleep again. When I went to hug her good-bye, I noticed that blood was creeping out from under her bandages, so I rang the buzzer for the nurse. The room was starting to smell a lot like Cherry Pride.

I didn't see much of Delphine after that day in the hospital. She began going to these religious meetings at the church hall every Friday night. She used me as an alibi the odd time, begged me to tell her parents we'd been hanging out together at the 7-Eleven. Really, I was down at the carving shed with Billy almost every evening.

But I never betrayed her secret. Wherever she is now, whoever she has become, I'd like her to know that. I never told a soul.

Mad as Sheela

Anita Rau Badami

IT WAS SUMMER, I was fifteen years old, and Madness was arriving at our place to ruin our holidays. Again. She had come every holiday since I was an infant. Other people traveled to see the Taj Mahal, or to mountain resorts such as Shimla to beat the scorching heat, but we went nowhere. How could we travel with a lunatic in tow?

She was my father's sister, and although she had a perfectly decent name—Sheela—all of us called her Madness. My mother, who hated having her around more than anyone, used a term in her mother-tongue, Kannada—*hùtch-mùnday*.

"The *hutch-mùnday* is coming," she would say angrily, as a prelude to an argument with our father. The term meant mad widow, which didn't really apply to Sheela Aunty. She was not a widow, nor had she ever married. She had told me, in one of her calmer moments, that she would like to get married—to a horse with a nice smile. She was particular about the teeth. She liked white, straight teeth, she said. I didn't know whether she was joking or whether she truly wanted to marry a handsome horse. It was sometimes difficult to tell with her. Later, however, I discovered that she was trying to be contemporary and young in her use of language. What she meant was that she wanted to marry a stud. She had found the word in a film magazine full of lurid gossip about Bombay movie stars and then forgotten it, remembering only that it had something to do with horses.

Dad had bought her a stack of these magazines, which she adored, much to my mother's irritation. As if it wasn't enough that we had Madness staying under our roof, ruining our summer vacations! Now my father was busy spending hard-earned money on this crazy sister of his. If any of us was particularly argumentative, moody, or obstreperous, Mummy would give that child a bitter look and hiss with fear-laden satisfaction, "I knew it! You are as mad as Sheela. Same family, what could I expect?" And then she would burst into wild tears at the thought that the errant, unpredictable gene that had wormed its way into my aunt's system had found a home in one of us as well.

I WAS THE OLDEST OF THREE CHILDREN. My father was an officer in the Indian Railways, and we lived in railway colonies in various parts of the country, depending on where Daddy's postings took us. The colonies were marked by a finely defined class system. Senior officials like my father lived in large bungalows at one end—typically the area with the oldest and shadiest trees, right across the road from the club where we could go to play badminton, tennis, or billiards, or to swim in the enormous pool, a luxury in a land parched for want of water in hot summer months. The size and condition of houses deteriorated as you went further down the ladder, to the homes of the men who were clerks or secretaries or engine drivers. In such a status-conscious, small society, everything was subject to scrutiny and gossip. My mother constantly warned me to behave myself, to dress neatly, to comb my hair every time a strand was out of place, to speak clearly and intelligently with my hands linked in front of me as if I were taking part in an elo-cution contest. Hundreds of little rules that drove me crazy! How was I to remember them all? By nature I was a dreamy, messy girl, less interested in my appearance than in getting to the club library to grab the latest books before anybody else got them. I said things without thinking, earning a glare from my mother. Sometimes I would catch her looking at me broodingly, and then she would say, "Why do you run around so much in the sun? Look at you, can't see the difference between your hair and your face!" I was skinny with a long nose in a thin, eager face, and my knees were always pocked with drying scabs acquired when I tumbled off my bicycle—which was very often. I ate my nails as if I were an addict, frantically, greed-ily, and without stopping.

If I was my mother's despair, my brother was the cat-astrophic middle child. He was thin and shy and, unlike me, never opened his mouth. This should have made my mother relieved; after all, she spent most of her time panicking about the next faux pas I would make. Instead, she compared my brother to the sons of some other railway wives and found him wanting. Those boys were loud, boisterous, and obnoxious, all signs that they would do well in life. Their energetic posturing showed that they had confidence, while my brother's retiring nature was an indication of his lacklustre future. Mummy was certain that those other boys had turned out that way because their mothers were not Working Women like her.

The railway wives either taught at the local school or belonged to the Women's Organization that put up fetes to collect money for charity, or held badminton tournaments or fancy-dress parties for the children. Working women were considered to be slightly inferior. My mother's employment revealed to everyone that neither she nor my father had family wealth to dip into. In an attempt to live down her notoriety, she became ferocious in her attempts to make sure that she had impeccable children. My sister, the youngest of the three, got away with everything, though. By the time she arrived, Mummy was too exhausted from trying to mold my brother and me into the children she read about in magazines, and of course, from dealing with the problem called Sheela Aunty.

Sheela was our shameful secret. Living as we did in a society that set so much store by appearances, rules of behavior, and status, we had no idea how to present her. If people knew that we had a lunatic for an aunt, they might not want to be acquainted with us, my mother said ominously, swearing my sister, my brother, and me to silence. "And once they know there will be no stopping them. They will tell everybody all over the country, and then in a few years, when it is time for you" (she would point her beautiful, sharp-nailed finger at me, the oldest daughter) "for you to get married, not even a fruit-seller from the village will want you." Nobody would give us jobs or come near us, she warned, just in case the madness that ran in our family had infected us.

And so we started lying to friends and visitors about the woman with the wild hair and unpredictable eyes who lived in the room right at the back of the house. She was a poor relative, or the daughter of a friend who could not afford to keep her, and so she was passed around from home to home like an unwanted parcel. She was a woman who had lost her family in a terrible accident and was recuperating from the shock. This implied that in the near future she would get over her loss and get back her mind. People understood tragedies; they sympathized with the victims. Thankfully, my father's job took us to a different city every three years, and so the Sheela lie could be maintained indefinitely.

The servants in the house, however, were a different matter. They traveled with us on every transfer and were privy to all kinds of family secrets. At first, they too were told that Sheela was a bereaved mother. But year after year, when Sheela turned up *still* crazy, my mother fostered the rumor that she was now irrevocably possessed by the ghosts of her lost children and there was no curing her of it.

My mother's own family, solid, unimaginative, financially stable, had no stain of madness, poverty, brilliance, or eccentricity to mar their existence. Daddy's, on the other hand, had a long history of strangeness attached to its name. In addition to Sheela Aunty, there was the bachelor uncle who was so handsome and well-off there could be only one reason for his unmarried status: he must be a homosexual. There was the great-uncle whose calling as an artist refused to allow him to work at anything. He drew pictures on the pavement because he had no money for art materials and had to support a wife and two daughters. In short, he was a beggar obliged to live on the money people threw out of pity on his street pictures. There were others, aunts so tall and thick-voiced they looked like eunuchs, and other aunts so ravishingly beautiful they must be whores. My paternal grandfather was a spendthrift who died of mouth cancer (another illness that was supposed to be bad for the family reputation), and his wife was an intellectual who spent all his pension money on books instead of saving it for her children. There was a drunkard, a cousin who had committed the crime of marrying a Muslim even though she was a high-caste Hindu, and an assortment of uncles who smoked and drank.

What a family, what a family! No wonder Mummy was in a state of anxiety about her children, who had such a heritage of oddness running through their genes. No wonder my father, who had imbibed all this strangeness with his mother's milk, didn't give a hoot what people thought of him or his family. How people must have laughed at us—

my father making no attempt to hide his relationship to Sheela Aunty, and my mother bending over backwards to protect us from the taint of that same relationship.

SHEELA WAS THE FOURTH SISTER in a family of twelve siblings. My father was the oldest son. He was twenty-three when his parents died and he inherited the responsibility of looking after the rest of the family. Although my grandfather had been a senior officer in the Indian Railway, his salary was enough to keep the family comfortable only as long as he was alive. Afterwards, my father and his younger brother, both of whom had just found jobs, were obliged to share the financial burden. The unwritten law of Indian relationships demanded that the oldest son take care of unmarried sisters for as long as he or they lived. And so Sheela Aunty came to us every summer.

Nobody was sure when our aunt went crazy. From all accounts she was fine until she turned nineteen, and then suddenly something happened to drive her over the edge. Some of my father's siblings claimed that Sheela lost her mind six months after her father's death, when her mother had also died in a spectacular way. Sheela had gone to the cinema with Grandmother, who suffered a brain hemorrhage in the theater. Successive tellings turned this event into a lurid drama with my grandmother convulsing and spewing blood from nose, mouth, and ears onto Sheela Aunty before she collapsed in the dark theater.

The theory offered by one of Sheela's younger brothers was that she had lost her mind after failing mathematics in her final year of university. She was apparently a genius until then and always got 100 percent in math.

"She couldn't take the shock of realizing that she was ordinary like the rest of us," my uncle would say sorrowfully, puffing away at his nth cigarette of the day, stroking his fingers through his shiny black hair. He was a dandy and made no pretence of being good at studies, although he admired people who were clever. He avoided Sheela Aunty, unable to reconcile his idea of her as a genius with her reincarnation as madwoman of the family.

Since her math exam had been a month after her mother's death, it was likely that her madness was the result of both traumatic experiences—the loss of her mother, and of her sense of being someone special.

An older cousin told me in later years that Sheela Aunty had been a fashionable young woman who wore clothes that matched exactly and suited her rich, dark coloring. She was fond of jewelry and carefully coordinated her earrings and bracelets with her saris. In an old family photograph, Sheela stands silently beside her mother, a faint smile playing about her full, shapely mouth. She is petite and very pretty. She has gentle eyes and thin, shapely fingers that she holds loosely knit in front of her. For the photo, she is wearing a checked sari and a blouse with puffed sleeves that was trendy at the time. Her hair is loosely braided and spills long and sinuous over one shoulder. There is another photograph with a few other siblings where she is smiling widely. She doesn't look like a Family Secret in either of those pictures.

IN THE EARLY 1950S, when my aunt went crazy, psychiatry was still in its infancy in India. There were lunatic asylums in remote towns and on the outskirts of large cities, but they were shrouded in mystery and generally avoided by "respectable" people. Only destitutes put members of their family there. Only lower-class people were seen entering those gates dragging drooling, screaming men or women. It wasn't a place for families like ours—high-caste Brahmins with a long history of illustrious ancestors, doctors, lawyers, civil servants, even a great-uncle who was a knight of the British Empire. *We* kept our lunatics and our sick people and our useless layabouts carefully wrapped up and locked in our cupboards with the other shameful secrets. An asylum was that dreadful place where angry mothers threatened to dump their errant children. It was believed that even the doctors in those institutes were not quite right in the head.

As far as my mother was concerned, our father had betrayed her and our family in the worst possible way by releasing Sheela Aunty from the Family Secret cupboard. The betrayal began on their wedding day. My father, claimed Mummy, had never bothered to mention his crazy sister until *after* he had tied the *mangal-sutra,* the marriage beads, around her slender throat. "Along with this," she said bitterly once, jerking the long chain of gold and black beads that hung down the slope of her breasts, "along with this, your father tied his sister around *my* neck."

On her worst days Sheela would mutter and glower, twist her fingers into knots, tear at her clothes ceaselessly, and roam like a caged animal in her room or out on the verandah. She wouldn't bathe until my mother forced her into the shower, and even after that stayed disheveled in a nightgown that was sometimes unbuttoned, revealing her bra and her naked belly. Even though Sheela Aunty and my mother were similarly built—slender women with narrow waists and taut, muscular arms, Sheela's madness gave her an unexpected strength. She fought my mother, screaming obscenities and trying to scratch Mummy's soft, heart-shaped face, which was distorted with a determination to get Aunty into the bathroom no matter what. If we hadn't been so terrified of both women, we might have found these slapstick episodes hilarious.

As if being dirty weren't bad enough, Sheela picked violently at her scalp and at insect bites until they bled. Then she picked at the scabs till the tiny bites became wounds. She would sit outside in full view of our neighbors and pull up her sari to scratch at her thin hairy legs. Sometimes she sang Hindi film songs from the fifties in a high off-key voice, the tunelessness drilling into our brains like the whine of a mosquito.

There were days when Sheela Aunty raged and became violent. Once, when I was about four years old, she stood watching me from her room as I sat at the dining table scribbling something on a piece of paper. My mother sat beside me, reading aloud from a book. Aunty, who was busy running an iron over a sari of hers, was unusually silent. She liked ironing things, even though she ironed randomly, creating creases with the hot metal on the cloth.

All of a sudden, Mother pushed me off my chair so hard that I fell to the floor, and then took a dive under the table herself. There was a crash. When we got up, me too startled even to holler, we found the iron lying near the wall, which had lost some of its paint from the impact. Aunty stood at the door of her room snickering softly to herself.

"Dirty girl," she said, gazing at me, and her eyes impenetrable. Staring up at her, I couldn't tell whether she was angry with me or not. "*Naughty* dirty girl," she said softly and then shut the door in our faces.

As a child I was afraid of Sheela Aunty, and it was only later, when I was in my teens, that she became an embarrassment. By that time, my mother's insistence on appearances had become a part of who I was. There was no hiding my mad aunt. She was my idea of misery. "Am I supposed to pretend that she is a figment of everybody else's imagination? Act as if she isn't ours? What? What?" I demanded of my mother once in a frenzy of tears.

A boy I wanted to impress, and who thought that I had beautiful eyes, had discovered that we had a madwoman in the house and didn't want to come over any more. He must have thought that craziness was an infectious disease. Sometimes I felt that way, too. There were days when I would cry passionately for no particular reason. The tears appeared irrationally and in vast quantities. Was this a sign of approaching madness? On other days, I was moody and quarrelsome and hated everyone in the house, even the cat that sat sunning itself contentedly on the verandah.

My mother I hated more than anyone else, because she

always seemed to be watching me for signs of the Sheela disease. If I were to lose my mind, I told Mummy once when I caught her staring speculatively at me as I lounged wide-legged on the living room couch, it would be *because* of her.

"Sit properly," my mother snapped. "Everyone can see your underwear. What will they think?" There was nobody else in the room, but the ghost of Other People sat between the two of us, leering at my knee-length bloomers.

Quite often when my friends were visiting, Sheela Aunty would materialize like a malevolent spirit at the door of my room. She would stand there motionless, her mouth churning without sound as if she was muttering spells at us.

"Who is she?" my friends would whisper, disconcerted by her dark stare, her unhappy, angry face.

"Someone from my dad's village," I would shrug. "She's very poor and my dad promised her family that we would look after her in the summer."

"Is she crazy?"

"Sort of. She went mad because her own family died." I would revert to the old lie, hoping that it was sticky enough to hold, convincing enough to be believed.

Of course, sooner or later, the truth would leak out. Sheela was my aunt. We had a madwoman in our family. And my friends would make excuses not to visit me. Their mothers would look pityingly or curiously at me when I went over to their homes, or ask embarrassing questions about Sheela. "What happened to her?" "Are there more mad people on your father's side?" "Was she born like that?"

My father treated his sister with a gentle patience. She was usually calm and well behaved when he was around, which sometimes made my mother wonder whether the mad behavior was an act put on to attract attention.

THE YEAR I TURNED SEVENTEEN, a large new hospital for the mentally ill opened in Bangalore city, where some of Dad's siblings lived. A relative who was a doctor pulled a few strings and made arrangements for Sheela Aunty to stay in the residential wing, as an employee and a patient. She appeared to be happy there, even though only a few of her siblings ever visited her. Her summer visits to our home became thankfully brief, because now she was an employee and couldn't take off for two entire months. She was also under medication, and as a result appeared to be much calmer. I started studying at a college in the same city, living on campus as a resident student. All my other aunts visited or had me over for the weekend, but Sheela Aunty was still an unmentionable fact of our family life.

At the hospital, Sheela Aunty learned a variety of skills, including weaving, knitting, and sewing. She sent long rambling letters addressed only to Dad, full of complaints about various staff members and gossip about other patients. The letters were penned in the most elegant copperplate script I had ever seen, smooth and flowing as black silk embroidery. If it weren't for the elusive language, the erratic thoughts, one might never have guessed that Sheela was ill at all.

When Dad died several years later, Sheela was devastated. She was the only sibling who didn't come to the funeral. She wrote us one last letter—addressed to my mother—offering condolences as if to a stranger. Accompanying the letter was a boxed ripe mango. "For your children," she wrote in that beautiful handwriting. There was no explanation for why she thought the fruit would fill the gap that Dad had left in our lives.

Sheela Aunty died a few months later of edema of the brain. She was alone when it happened. I hardly thought about her again until I started working on my first novel. And then, in a burst of color and noise, our family secret came out of the shadows. The aunt who had been larger and more ghastly than life had finally found a home that suited her perfectly—in fiction.

Dancing with My Father

Lorna Crozier

THERE'S A PHOTOGRAPH OF MY DAD and me the night of my grade twelve graduation. I'm in my first long dress, a sleeveless, aqua peau de soie with small covered buttons spilling down the right side. For the first time in my life, I have a hairdo. Ginnie at the local shop has shaped my curls into a bundle of sausage rolls on top of my head. Later, I'll groan every time I look at my hair in this photo. Now, I think it's as sophisticated as anything I'd see in a *Movietone* magazine.

Dad is wearing his only suit. It's the same kind most prairie men of his background and generation save for weddings and funerals, ignoring the shifts in fashion or their body shape. His arm drapes across my shoulders and, as he turns from me to the camera, his sloppy grin looks as if it's about to slide off his face. Before Mom snaps the picture, he says, "You're my little girl."

In the photograph our feet don't show. Mine are in satin high heels dyed the same color as my dress. He's wearing his good "oxfords," as they were called. Mel Caswell's wife gave them to him when Mel died. They were both small men with small feet, but every time Dad wears the shoes he complains that they pinch. If you could see the oxfords in the photograph, you'd notice that the laces are undone. After the picture, Mom, in a snit, sits Dad on the couch, yanks the laces and knots a bow. He leans on her as we walk to the door.

We're close to being late for the banquet in the school gym a few blocks away. We *have* to be on time; I'm the valedictorian, and my family is supposed to sit with the principal at the head table, where I'll give my speech after everyone's consumed the ham, scalloped potatoes, and jellied salads. Over coffee and apple pie, my fellow grads and their parents will listen to my optimistic, conservative lines about the values our elders have taught us and how these will guide us through the years to come. There's no sense of teenaged angst, no disrespect or rebellion in my speech, no true words about what I've learned from my father. Although it's 1966, it's small-town Saskatchewan, and the sixties are happening somewhere else.

The night before the graduation ceremony, Mom and I knew there'd be trouble when Dad didn't come home. He didn't stay away overnight all that often, but when he did we knew he'd fallen into a poker game, probably at someone's farm, or a heavy drinking party that didn't know how to end. "It's always when something important is happening that he acts like this," my mom said. The last big public event in the family had been my brother's wedding two years before. The three of us had caught the night train from Swift Current to Winnipeg where my brother was stationed in the air force, Dad with a bottle in his suit jacket, shouting and singing, keeping everyone awake until the porter threatened to throw him off. Shame was a large part of living with him, but that was the first time I willed myself to grow small, so small that no one could see me. Later, I was startled when I caught the reflection of my face in the window of the train. I thought I had made myself disappear.

The afternoon of my graduation, my mom made me walk to the school to tell Mr. Whiteman, the teacher in charge, that my father wouldn't be at the banquet. He'd been called out of town for work, I was to say. The story was implausible, because my father's job was in the oil fields, just a few miles away. I prayed that Mr. Whiteman didn't know what Dad did for a living, and I squirmed at the thought of lying to him. He was my English teacher, I'd just gotten 97 percent on my Easter exam, and I wanted to keep his respect.

Mr. Whiteman nodded his head and said nothing, but I saw something in his gaze that I'd never seen before. It wasn't disappointment or anger. Would I have known then to call it pity? Whatever it was, it made me mad, not at my parents or myself, but at him. The love I felt for my father was fierce. It would have been easier if I could have simply hated him.

Now, a few hours later, I walk ahead of my parents to the school to relay the good news that my father is able to make it after all. The head table will need to be rearranged, my father's placecard set beside mine. Trying to get to the gym before the other grads and their parents are seated, I walk as fast as I can, pounding my new thin heels so hard on the sidewalk that the rubber tip breaks off my right shoe. Mr. Whiteman is standing by the stage I helped decorate the day before with crêpe paper streamers, Kleenex roses, and balloons. When I move between the long tables across the floor towards him, one shoe makes a clicking noise; the other lands without a sound. I wish anything would happen but what's about to. I wish I were any other place on earth.

IN OUR SMALL CROWDED LIVING ROOM a few weeks before graduation, my father and I are dancing. He is good on his feet, gliding me through an old-time waltz, a two-step, a quicker fox-trot. My toes stub into his. No matter how many times he tells me to relax, my body stiffens. At the Friday night Teen Town dances, I have no trouble with grace and daring. I twist and jive with the best of them, and I'm a master of my generation's kind of waltz: my partner and I stand almost still, swaying, arms wrapped tightly around sweaty backs as if we're keeping each other afloat. Heads bobbing above the dark, we swoon to music we barely hear above the warm rush of blood and heartbeat. But my parents' kind of dancing—the two slow backward steps followed by two fast ones forward, the smooth slide through circles, the quick crossing of the floor, avoiding the couch, the chair, the big console radio–record player combination—requires more coordination than I've been born with.

My father is gentle with me; he is patient. When I can make myself relax, I follow him with a minimum of awkwardness. My feet only have to be smart enough to get us through one dance—the first of the evening, which all the grads have to endure with one of their parents. And it doesn't really matter what condition Dad might be in. Drunk or not, one of his finest skills is that he can make it around a dance floor without stumbling. His feet never slur.

MY MOTHER NEVER SPEAKS about my father's drunkenness to anyone but me, and I've been warned repeatedly not to tell my friends. His drinking is our skeleton in the closet, our mad child hidden in the attic. The bones rattle, the feet bang on the floor above our heads, but if someone else is around, we pretend not to hear.

"What goes on in the family stays in the family," Mom says. "It's no one else's business." It isn't that she's hiding any kind of physical or sexual violence—no matter how much my father drinks or how angry he seems, he never hits her or me. He's never abused us. She's simply covering up embarrassing behavior, like the time he woke up in the middle of the night and peed in his shoe. Why tell anyone about that? Or the time he tripped on an imaginary branch on the sidewalk and came home with his nose scraped and bleeding and his glasses broken. Or the nights he spent in jail. Her insistence on privacy has something to do with pride. She is honest and hardworking, and she wants, in spite of our family's poverty and my dad's bad behavior, to hold her head up high.

I understand the reasons for her silence, but I suffer terribly from it. What our secret means in practical terms is that I can't invite my friends home after school or ask them to stay for supper. I can't take my turn at hosting sleepovers where my buddies and I dance to records in our babydoll pajamas, suck back bowls of chips and Cheezies, and stay up all night talking about boys. I can't tell anyone the real reason why Mom and I walk everywhere: Dad's too inebriated to drive, or he's lost his license and then his job operating heavy machinery in the oil patch. I can't tell my boyfriend why I don't ask him to spend Christmas with my family when he's left alone, his parents responding to a relative's death a thousand miles away. What do I tell him? Another lie.

I'm essentially an honest kid. Having to lie is a burden, but the worst effect of our secret is that it forces me to hide my sadness. I bury it beneath an exterior that has little to do with what is going on at home and with how I see myself in my mind's mirror. My cheerful, outgoing double sings in the school operettas, captains the cheerleading team, serves on the executive of Teen Town, teaches swimming lessons, acts in the drama nights, goes steady with boys, worries about how far a good girl should go, and never speaks of anything that matters. On the surface, I am well-adjusted, popular, optimistic. Inside I burn with shame. My father's drinking is such a disgraceful thing that it can't be talked about. It has to be carried invisibly like a terrible disease that has no name.

MY FATHER NEVER LIES about his drinking. What would be the point? But I never hear either of my parents use the word *alcoholic*. He drinks, but he claims he can hold his liquor. That ability is part of being a man, as is his right to spend his paycheck on anything he wants. As is his prowess at arm-wrestling, shuffleboard, and pool. The windowsills in our living room shine with trophies he's brought home from the bars. They compete for space with the curling trophies he and Mom have won as skips of their own teams, though that game's prizes are often more practical—matching table lamps, a big wine-colored ottoman made out of Naugahyde, a set of cutlery, a side of beef.

For Mom, his excess isn't a disease; it stems from selfishness and a lack of affection for us. "He cares more about the Legion," she says. "He'd rather be with a bunch of drunks than his family." If he isn't an alcoholic, if he can stop whenever he wants to, the deficiencies are ours, not his.

I'm not good enough or pretty enough or smart enough to keep him home. Nor is she. He seems to be having a good time, at least until he has to face her anger every morning before he leaves for work. She and I are the ones full of shame and anxiety and despair. We're the ones sitting at home each night, dreading his arrival, hoping we'll be in bed and can pretend to be asleep when he stumbles in the door.

My father's drinking and the taboos surrounding it draw my mother and me closer together. She tells me her troubles because she can tell no one else, and she becomes more and more independent. Sometimes she doesn't keep his supper warm when he's late; sometimes we're out when he gets home. It's easy to believe that she and I are the only ones who live in the house. My father is an unwelcome, troublesome relative who drops in from far away, demanding and unannounced. He takes us for granted, and he never gives my mother enough money to run the house without her having to beg.

The year I turned fourteen, my mother got a job selling tickets at the Junior A Bronco hockey games. The rink was on the outskirts of town, a couple of miles from our house. She didn't have a driver's licence and couldn't rely on my dad to show up sober or on time, so she walked all winter through the dark and cold to the evening games. Sometimes she'd get a ride home with a fellow worker; if not, she'd make the trek on foot back again. I can still see her small bundled figure trudging through the snow, the icy wind whipping around her. When I call up the memory, it's as if I'm watching her from high above and she's the only moving thing in all that white.

She and I had set off on similar walks together when I was little. Once, after we'd waited for an hour for Dad to pick us up from the Eagles' Christmas party, a brown bag of hard, striped candy clutched in my hand, we headed out down the dark and snowy streets alone. Mom had refused offers of other rides. The temperature had fallen to thirty below, and she couldn't believe he wouldn't come. Halfway home, because I was shivering, she undid the big buttons on her old muskrat coat and pulled me inside, the back of my head pressing into her belly, the satin lining slipping across my forehead and nose. What strange tracks we must have printed in the snow as I blindly shuffled my feet between hers.

Sunday afternoons my father spent drinking in the Eagles' lounge. When it closed, he came home with a Fat Emma or Pie Face chocolate bar for Mom and me, and after supper we'd eat them watching *The Ed Sullivan Show* on our first television set, a big, wooden Fleetwood in the center of the living room. A scrawny eight-year-old, I'd sit by Dad on the couch, as close as I could get, to play what he called "wrestling," and I secretly called "the hand-hurting game." I'd bend back his thumbs until he cried uncle. I'd push the flesh of his fingertips over his closely bitten nails. This would go on for the whole hour, me trying to hurt my father. I delighted in our physical closeness, and he seemed to like my needy aggression, telling me how strong I was and pretending to be in pain. At the time I thought his cries of injury were real. I was always the one who initiated the game, and he patiently let me maul his fingers until I decided to stop.

Harming them became my way of touching him and of having him touch me.

In some ways I envy the kid I was back then, because

I wanted my father around. I knew that I loved him and he loved me. Home less often now, even on a Sunday night, he is drinking more. When he's with us in front of the TV, I don't sit beside him. Soon I'm the one who is gone, flying out the front door at the honk of horn, driving around with whoever has a car, meeting the rest of my friends at the A&W and horsing around.

I don't touch my father again until our dancing lessons a few weeks before graduation. Part of my clumsiness, my slowness to learn, is his sudden, unavoidable closeness. I can smell the beer on his breath, feel the occasional brush of whiskers on my cheek, the heat of his hand holding mine, and the weight of his other hand in the small of my back. When I am able to relax even a little, there is also a pleasure in being in the circle of his arms.

During the grad banquet and my speech, my father's head nods, and his mouth droops open. My mother elbows him now and then so he won't pass out completely and start to snore. After the plates are cleared away, the tables folded and pushed to the sides of the gym, the band leader in his red jacket and black pants announces "the grad-parents' waltz," and my father and I walk to the center of the floor. It is one of the valedictorian's duties to lead this dance. For a few minutes we are the only two people in the world. We are standing on an ice floe, cold and drifting, observed by hundreds of eyes. I am so afraid that something awful is about to happen, that my father will fall, that he'll say something loud about how pretty I look and everyone will hear, that the principal will have to walk across the floor and lead us off.

Everything is still and quiet. I can see my mother watching from the sidelines. Then the music starts; I slide my feet to the practiced steps my father has taught me. The other grads and their parents rise from their chairs and swirl among us. For a moment, I lose sight of my mother's nervous smile. I let myself go limp and move automatically at the slightest pressure of his hands. We never speak or stumble. The song ends, and we've made it through as if we were normal, as if this were an easy ordinary task. I thank my father, walk him to my mother at the edge of the onlookers and find my date. We watch my parents dance one waltz; then, her arm in his, my mother leads my father to the door to take him home.

Most of the other adults stay for the first half of the dance and either waltz together or watch their kids' gyrations from the sidelines. I'm ecstatic I'm alone with the boy I'll be with for just this special night. A fellow grad, he's not a boyfriend, though we dance close and later, at the wiener roast ten miles south of town, we neck in the front seat of his older brother's car. Not once in the evening do we mention my father. Not once do we say the word "drunk." I'm starting to believe that somehow a glass cocoon lowers around my father after his first few beer. His loudness, his weave and stumble, the sloppiness of his smile are hidden behind the glass as long as my mother and I don't talk about him. When we keep quiet, only we can see or hear him. To everyone else, he's invisible.

Except, perhaps, when the two of us are dancing. Earlier

that evening, we glided in our best shoes across the polished gym floor. Past my classmates and their parents, all of them watching, all of them thinking for the length of a song that we looked good together, this father, this daughter, moving in slow, perfect time in each other's arms.

There Will Be No Secrets

Almeda Glenn Miller

WHEN I WAS REALLY YOUNG my dad whispered to me a lot. He'd take me aside and tell me secrets. Sometimes the secrets were plots to overthrow the government; other times they were plots to overthrow my mom. Mom didn't like it when my dad whispered. She thought it was dishonest.

Dad was adamant about his privacy. He loved to smoke his pipe and read into the wee hours. He'd watch us wrestle from behind the Saturday newspaper or hide away in his study while we tiptoed around the house protecting him from us. He would tell me how shy he'd always been, and how tough it was for him to walk into a room full of people, him being six feet, five inches tall, dark-skinned and wearing an eye patch. "Try to be unassuming," he'd say, "when you are one of the monocular minority." I understood that he might be a shy, private man, so to expose his family to the public failure of his marriage seemed inconsistent.

I had thought it was my mom's fault when my parents split up. But a friend of my mom's, a woman we called Aunty Denise, tried to set me straight one evening. Mom was inside preparing dinner. Mom's friend and I stood along the fence line of our property, an acreage south of town that my parents had bought when they thought a change of scenery might make their marriage better. It was cool enough for me to be wearing a sweater, and I was brushing down Trixy, the twenty-year-old horse my parents had given me for my eleventh birthday. Her tawny smell mixed in the air with the dank odor of freshly swathed alfalfa. The blanket and saddle were poised on the fence post.

I was just about to remove Trixy's bridle and take everything into the barn when Aunty Denise began to inventory my dad's infidelities, the way he had hit on everybody from my mom's sister to a long list of secretaries, business associates, and most of my mom's close friends. One of them—her name was June—he had been seen with only the other day. The sun was low in the sky, so Aunty Denise's face was soft, her eyes moist and meaningful as she patted me on the shoulder, then walked away. My sweater caught and ripped on the barbed-wire fence as I grabbed the saddle and blanket.

That summer when I turned eleven and my parents split up, my mom started dating different guys. She had taken a job at a cheesy motel/bar in town. She hadn't worked for years—she was a nurse by trade—and this was the only job she could get. One night, after my dad took my brothers and me to a movie, we sat in the driveway of our home with the car idling. I was telling my dad all sorts of stuff because I didn't want him to leave. We were each other's confidantes. He always said we saw the world the same way. After my brothers got out and ran in front of the headlights, their plaid jackets blurred by the speed of their escape, Dad leaned over and whispered into my ear: "Find out how your mom is spending her money and who she is spending her time with." I was my father's special agent. I was the only one of us that could be trusted with this mission. I lay in bed that night and dreamed of ways I could save my dad.

I don't know why I thought he needed to be saved, but the following day over breakfast I asked Mom where she was spending her money and who she was spending her time with. She told me that it was none of my business. She kissed all three boys on their foreheads but she just squeezed my shoulder, not even tightly, when she left the breakfast table. Later that same morning I sneaked into my mom's room and telephoned Dad to report to him, and when I heard Mom pick up the telephone in the study I screamed into the receiver and then didn't say anything— for the next three months. I completely stopped talking. I stopped eating and walking, too. My three brothers thought I was retarded. When Mom and Dad came to visit me in the hospital, they argued at my bedside about which one of them was to blame.

Truth is, I was faking it. I could have walked or talked or eaten anytime I wanted, but not doing so seemed to be the only way to stop the espionage. As part of my rehabilitation, I built a lampshade out of Styrofoam cups, played cards with the hydrocephalic in the bed next to me, and babysat the cute little boy down the hallway whose esophagus had been burned out from drinking Drano. Slumped in my wheelchair for hours in the psychiatrist's office, I picked at the woven fabric of my hospital blanket, and tugged at the tape around my intravenous tube while he discussed important issues with his interns. When they finally released me into my mother's care, the psychiatrist told her I was uncommunicative but probably not a danger to myself. I overheard my dad murmuring to Mom that I was just being dramatic."

During my stay in the hospital, Mom and Dad finalized their divorce, had a custody battle—Mom won—and Mom and the boys moved into town. Mom had enrolled in a refresher course and then landed a head nurse position at a hospital on the north end of town. As I requested, she had painted my bedroom black, laid red shag carpet down, and given me my own phone line. It was only after I moved in that she let me remove all the bedroom furniture so I could crash out on the floor in a sleeping bag. "You want to feel like a tourist for a while?" she asked me. "Fine," she said, "for a while, and then I want my girl back."

DAD MARRIED JUNE on New Year's Eve. Mom says he did that for income tax purposes. Now we go to his place on the weekends. He and June and June's five kids live in a luxurious house in the wealthy part of town. We play bridge in the evenings and read, and in an odd way the quiet of the house is a welcome respite from the chaos of Mom's home. At my father's, there are locks on all the doors and rooms we aren't allowed to enter. There is furniture we are forbidden to sit on and certain dishes in the cupboard we aren't allowed to use. We aren't to go into the fridge, and there is to be no snacking between meals. There are polished silver napkin rings with the names of June's children engraved on them. There aren't any for my brothers and me.

My dad's new wife is a ghostly rail of a woman with elegant posture and a quiet, private nature. His new children are intelligent, even-tempered people who whisper in the hallways and wear parlor clothes, clothes that are strictly for lounging around the house. The girls apply their makeup thickly and wear their hair combed over their faces. Their voluminous dresses reach to the floor and hide their bodies. The boys are kind and considerate, but think themselves more refined than my brothers and me. It is a polite household, something like what I imagine finishing school must be. My dad's wife sits with her back straight, knees together, and ankles crossed. We call her "June." Her kids call my father "Mr. C." Mr. C sleeps in a separate bedroom from June, but one of my stepsisters assures me they get it on some nights when they think nobody else is awake.

Late on a Sunday afternoon, my father whispers because he wants me to pay attention. We sit in the den of their beautiful home, a forest-green room walled with books, a fireplace, and two overstuffed chairs with matching ottomans, and he tells me that he wants my oldest brother and me to come and live with him, because we are the ones most like him. He conspires to split me from my other brothers. When I think about this I can't breathe. Dad leaves me alone in the den to retrieve the boys before Mom comes to pick us up. Between gasps, I scribble a poem about how much I ache for him to come back to us and how torn my skin feels—"The Very Rawness of Rupture," I think I title it—and when it is time to leave I hand him my heart on a piece of stationery. He folds, doubles, and folds my words into hushes, then stuffs them into his suit pocket.

When we walk to the car, he won't hold my hand. Sitting in the back seat of my mom's Chevy Impala, an interminable sadness blossoms inside me. I will do *none* of the leaving in this family. My parents argue because my mom has let me pierce my ears. I'm thinking how much I hate both of them. I'm totally choked, because I figure my ears are nobody's business but mine.

On Sunday night, on the other side of town, back at home, in the only place my mom can afford, we throw chocolate pudding at each other. My oldest brother starts it. He flicks a blob of pudding right onto my middle brother's T-shirt. My mom can't help herself and she dumps her entire bowl over my head. But when my little brother begins to huck spoonfuls at the kitchen cupboards, Mom scolds him for going too far. That's when my middle brother stuffs the pudding into my oldest brother's belly button and we all fall to the floor in hysterics. Later that same night, Mom holds us all as we cry ourselves to sleep.

AFTER ONE OF THESE DELIRIOUS SUNDAY EVENINGS, Mom removes the lock on the bathroom door in our house and declares, "There will be no secrets in this family."

The bathroom becomes our meeting ground, the place we all find ourselves in the morning before school or in the evening before bed. No lock on the door means that my older brother is brushing his teeth while I'm having a pee, or I'm braiding my hair while my younger brother is flossing. There is always the uncomfortable threat of someone bursting in on me while I am picking my zits.

My middle brother goes so far as to remove the doorknob to the bathroom. My little brother and I stand outside the door and shout at him to finish playing with himself so we can get ready for bed. He shoves a cloth in the peephole and we have to fetch a knife from the kitchen, stab it into the door mechanism, and twist it around several times until the door opens. This gives him enough time to zip up his pants.

My little brother is the one who lodges the formal complaint about the absence of a proper doorknob and lock. Before school one day, he tapes the toilet up with masking tape, weaves string back and forth in a spiderweb pattern across the outside frame of the bathroom door. He then pulls the door shut behind the string. Under any other circumstances, Mom would have considered this a valid artistic expression. But Mom has a bladder problem, on account of her having so many kids. She's been known to pull over during rush-hour traffic and pee into the gutter. When she has to go, nobody can stand in the way, not even the obstacle course my brother has built for her.

When Mom flies in from work, the four of us are sitting in the kitchen. We listen to her frantically tear at the string and pound her fists on the door. We wave at her as she scrambles into the kitchen to fetch a knife, run down the hall, jab the knife in the mechanism, open the door, rip at the tape to get at the toilet barely in time. "You little buggers," she bellows, laughing. After that episode, Mom reluctantly agrees to return the lock on our bathroom door. But she continues to leave the door ajar when she is in there, because she doesn't like to miss anything.

WITHIN A YEAR OF MOVING into our new home, Mom buys us a pool table, shuffleboard, and a dartboard for the basement. Every teenager in the community hangs out at our house. She coordinates an evening for a woman to come from the birth control clinic to discuss options with everybody. My mom scolds Sheila Cassidy's parents when they call the cops on her for showing pornographic images to minors. "Your daughter has already had one abortion; I am not going to let it happen again," Mom snaps into the telephone. She sticks her tongue out at the receiver and hangs up.

Other kids don't tell their parents anything. We tell our mom everything. If we don't, Mom always finds out. She catches my older brother and me hotknifing some hash in the basement. There's a healthy stain of resin on the deep freeze; a neatly broken vodka bottle sits on the shelf over the laundry room sink, and all the knives in the kitchen have tarnished tips. "Geez, I wonder how she found out," my sister mocks us. My sister is old enough to live on her own. She only visits to set us straight on a few things. But Mom doesn't punish us. She says she wants to try smoking marijuana with us sometime.

With no secrets in our new life, there is what seems a limitless frontier, an illusion of safety, like wearing water wings when you don't know how to swim. Should I smoke dope with angel dust in it or not? Should I drink the entire bottle of Southern Comfort or the whole case of beer? Should I take Mom's keys and drive my best friend home, even when I know I'm drunk and haven't got a driver's license? Should I lose my virginity on the new pool table in the basement while everyone is upstairs watching Captain Kirk seduce Yeoman Rand in the sick bay, or should I tell the boy I'm saving myself for love? I tell my mom everything, except about the angel dust debacle.

You can see why our friends adore her. They say she's hip, and obviously she lets us get away with a ton of stuff. We have to beg her to put her clothes on before our friends come over, though. They think her nudity is cool, but this public display mortifies my brothers and me. Mom has been sick lately and has lost a bit of weight, but her body is supple. She barely has any stretch marks from carrying five children, and even though she breast-fed all five of us, her breasts are quite pert. She is always walking around naked, talking on the phone, cooking dinner, and washing the dishes. It makes it difficult for my middle brother. He wants to smoke dope and party in the woods with his friends, but they just want to hang around my mom and watch her vacuum.

Mom can't monitor what my middle brother is doing when he isn't at home, and even though his friends want to hang out at our place he wants to be anywhere but home. Luckily, when he overdoses on acid, Mom is working emergency and is with him when he crashes.

Mom can't monitor what my oldest brother is doing because he's moved in with my dad and his new family. In as steady a voice as she can muster, Mom informs my brother on the telephone that if he's man enough to leave us then he's man enough to come for his own clothes. I am doing the laundry because it's my turn, and I find one of my oldest brother's shirts shoved under my mom's pillow. I write him a poem about his shirt, the way it smells. I call it, "Once We Were Seven, Now We Are Four." He shoves it into his jeans pocket.

Shortly after my oldest brother moves out, my dad sends a social worker over to investigate my mom. We don't know at first that this person is a social worker because my mom often has strangers in the house when we come home from school, people she has picked up hitchhiking, lost souls from the church, patients she has brought home from the hospital, ex-cons from the remand center where she volunteers. But we are polite teenagers who stop and visit in the kitchen before excusing ourselves. I go into the living room to practice my piano, my middle brother heads downstairs to practice his clarinet, and my little brother takes the social worker into his room to show off his comic book collection. My mother remains in the kitchen, running her fingers through her hair. She is trying to figure out how she is going to sleep before her night shift. This is the time she usually sleeps. She works night shift so she can be home to make us breakfast, "the most important meal of the day," according to her.

Mom invites the social worker to stay for dinner. We hold hands while we sing "Johnny Appleseed," and before we eat Mom always likes to say to guests, "If there's something you want but you can't see it on the table, just ask us and we'll tell you how to do without it." At the end of the evening, the social worker and Mom plan to meet under different circumstances as friends. Mom sends her off with a piece of the angel food cake that she baked from scratch.

THE YEAR I TURN FIFTEEN, Mom is the camp director at our Unitarian church summer camp. She greets newcomers wearing nothing but a crown made of birchbark. Everybody else's mom and dad walk around naked, too, so we don't feel so obvious. My brothers and I aren't that keen to go naked, even though Mom tells us that it is only natural. I don't like it when she sits in the sand with her legs parted and I can see where I came from. I just think there are places I don't want to go back to.

My mom thinks I am being uptight. She says I'm just like my dad, as if that is the worst insult she could ever give me. I spend most of the summer alone, wandering the backwoods, hanging by the creek, building myself safe places where nobody can dictate to me how to be. I begin to keep a journal of secrets I'll never share with my mom. Secrets about who I am and how I feel.

For my mom, secrets are the horrible dark things that selfish people whisper behind closed doors. They are the dangerous breeding grounds for deception. Secrets mock the vulnerable, gullible natures of the innocent. We are lying in our sleeping bags underneath the stars when she utters to me that her own mother used to beat her with a switch. Mom perches on a boulder by the falls and I am fishing in the pool below when she shouts across the crash of the current that her cousin was raped and left in the ditch by the crossroads. We are washing dishes when she confesses that the old fart at the hardware store in her hometown used to take her behind the counter and fiddle with her. Mom seizes me by the shoulders, scouring my eyes with hers. "These are the kinds of secrets," she implores, "that nobody should ever have to keep to themselves." I'm thinking that my secrets aren't so dangerous.

THERE ARE SOME THINGS my brothers and I have always known but never talk about. It never seemed important to us until my middle brother has this fight at school. He comes home swollen-lipped and bruised around one eye. Some of the kids were calling him a "Paki." I look at my brother. I mean, really look at him. He has these gorgeous brown eyes that sparkle when he teases me and high cheekbones that make him look particularly smart. He has a mole on the bridge of his nose—I never noticed that before. His hair is dark brown and he has curls that fall like shaved chocolate over his shoulders and down his back. His skin is the color of sandalwood, and we always joke about how he's so skinny he has to jump around in the shower to get wet. I can see his heart thrash against his ribs as he stands in the kitchen and Mom holds an ice pack on his cheekbone.

My mom says, "If you try to talk to your father about being East Indian, he'll tell you he's a Communist as well. He hates it when people try to label him as one thing or another, as if being East Indian or being Communist is anybody's business but his." My dad always says he's prejudiced against people who are prejudiced. And sometimes he thumps his fist so hard on the dinner table, the cutlery and glass clatter like music beneath his tirade against the injustice and arrogance of the British blue-blood. "The truth is," my mom rubs vitamin E over my brother's cheekbone, "he can't remember anything about his Indian mother because she died of malaria before he turned six. His father disinherited him, and he doesn't like anybody else in his family."

Later that night, my brother and I stare at each other. His fat lip has settled down a bit. His eyes are puffy from crying, but they are still brown, and his skin is brown, too. We compare the skin around our elbows. "You've got Paki elbows," he says to me. "You've got Paki ankles," I say to him. "You do, too." But I'm blonde and blue-eyed, and I have always been titillated by the fact that nobody knows what I have inside me.

Mom comes down to tuck us into bed. She says, "After his mother died, your father was sent away from his family to a British boarding school when he was six years old. The priests in the boarding school told him to say he was of Spanish extraction." She leans against the doorway. "The Spanish were such a convenient disguise for the Indian." She glances around the room, then leans in as if about to betray someone. "The Spanish, they liked to mix up the gene pool a bit." We continue to stare at her, and she becomes edgy. "When your father was a boy, it was more acceptable to have been raped by a Spaniard than to have been loved by an Indian." She inhales and shudders. "He was taught by priests to keep secrets. That's why he is such a cagey man." She kisses us both on our foreheads and leaves the room.

DAD CALLS ME his little "drama queen" every time I beg him to come back to us. I know he's remarried, but I keep hoping it's a mistake. Turns out I am a "drama queen" and a professional troupe hires me for a part I audition for. This means I kiss a guy on stage in a comedy called *Boeing Boeing*. It's about this guy who keeps several mistresses. Mom says the play is about "convergence" and she hopes my dad enjoys opening night. Dad refuses to come to the play because he says he doesn't want to see his little girl kissing anybody. I don't tell him that I French kiss on stage to make it look authentic and that I've been sleeping with the actor since rehearsals began.

Mom catches a whiff of the actor on me one night and wants to know every detail. She tells me that when she has an orgasm she can always smell orange groves. I fake my orgasms, so I have no hope of smelling oranges. What I don't share with my mom is that I wish I were still a virgin.

WHEN I TURN SIXTEEN, we find out that Mom has cancer. After a long series of tests, the doctor admits her to hospital. My dad mumbles an offer to take my little brother, but thinks that the three of us might be too much for June to handle. She is, after all, going through menopause. We tell my dad thanks but no thanks, that we'll do fine on our own. He is secretly relieved and so are we.

I visit Mom in the hospital every day after dance and before piano. The second I get off the elevator I can hear the familiar sound of a coyote caught in a leg trap. It is my mom, bawling. The nurses emerge from her room whispering to each other. They have had enough of her pain. When I steal in, she turns her reddened face toward me. Her dark hair clings to her forehead like wet leaves, and spiders of blood have spread beneath the skin of her cheeks. The bedclothes are tossed back and she is lying naked, a fierce red scar across her belly. Something round and swollen is clawing its way through her sutures. There is nothing sacred about this moment. I would give anything to forget this. There are no secrets here, no privacy, nothing personal, no public declarations, just my mother and me inside her pain. Over my mother's wails, I can no longer hear the conspiracy in my father's whispers. Both the conspiracy and my father are irrelevant in this place.

Suspended like a marionette, I dangle before the tall

windows of the room, my arm rises, and my hand draws aside the vertical blinds. The snow drifts across the highway below. The sky is white, the ground is white, and people are leaning into the blizzard with their eyes to the ground. Everything is stripped away. My arm drops to my side. For a moment—only a moment—I lose my mooring.

My mother is panting behind me. When I turn back, she pats her hand twice on the bed. I go to her and slip my hand into hers. Her fingers are strong and warm as she folds them deliberately around mine. She gives my hand a little shake and asks me if I have any secrets I want to share with her. I tell her I have no secrets, not right now.

About the Authors

ANITA RAU BADAMI is the author of two critically acclaimed novels: *Tamarind Mem* and *The Hero's Walk*. Both have been published in several countries. Her third novel will be out in fall 2004.

LORNA CROZIER did all kinds of dumb things as a teenager, including being a cheerleader, going "steady" with boys, wearing chest-hugging bras to make her breasts look smaller, and stealing stuff from Woolworths to see if she could get away with it. Poetry writing saved her life, and it still does. She lives in an old house with a big garden, plus two cats and a husband who also writes.

NAN GERMAINE has written for radio and magazines and has taught English literature at the college level. She lives on the eastern slopes of the Rocky Mountains, not far from where she grew up. Married with two children, she likes hiking and skiing.

ALMEDA GLENN MILLER's first novel, *Tiger Dreams,* was published in 2002. Her short fiction has appeared in *Dandelion, Glimmertrain Stories,* and *Willowsprings.* She is working on her second novel about love and forgiveness in the Middle East. Almeda Glenn Miller lives and writes in Rossland, British Columbia.

KELYS GREEN lives in Toronto, Canada, with her partner, two cats, and a parrot. She teaches English literature. Under another name, she sometimes writes fiction. Occasionally she's lucky enough to get some of it accepted for publication.

SUSAN MUSGRAVE is an award-winning author of poetry, critical writing, and adult and children's fiction. At age sixteen, her first poems were published in a literary journal. Her most recent collection of poetry is *What the Small Day Cannot Hold*, and her most recent novel is *Cargo of Orchids*. Susan has taught literature and writing, and has been writer-in-residence at several schools. Her home is on Vancouver Island.

CATHY STONEHOUSE emigrated to Canada from the U.K. in 1988. She lives in Vancouver, where she is editor of *Event*, a literary magazine, and has published a book of poetry, *The Words I Know.* She is currently working on a collection of short stories, tentatively entitled *People Like Us,* and a novel.

Going Crazy, Wanna Come?

Susan Musgrave

"I don't advocate drugs, alcohol, violence or insanity—but they've always worked for me."

I began my convocation speech to a high school graduating class several years ago by quoting the journalist Hunter S. Thompson. I said insanity was what had *kept* me sane throughout high school because, among other things, my teeth weren't straight enough for me to be a cheerleader. Most of the graduates I was addressing came from goal-oriented upper-middle-class families. "Forget about goals," I told them. "Sigmund Freud said death is the goal of all life. Sooner or later you'll all reach your goal, so try to live a little in the meantime." The teachers told me afterwards it was the first speech they'd ever seen their students listen to.

The next day twenty outraged parents phoned the principal to complain. I was pleased that, almost thirty years after I had dropped out of high school, I still had the ability to annoy so many parents. I figured I must be doing *something* right.

I've never been the kind of writer who believes she can change the world, but I've always believed it's a writer's job to shake things up, to disturb the status quo. My teachers used to tell me I had the wrong attitude. As far as I'm concerned, it's the only kind of attitude to have. I'm happy to say this particular principal supported me, which is more than my own high school principal had done. When I ended up in his office for necking with my boyfriend instead of paying attention in Biology, "the Monk" (as we called him because of the hair growing out of his ears) told me that if I continued on this downward spiral of kissing boys, writing poetry, and skipping classes, I would most likely end up as a prostitute. But I already knew the world's oldest profession wasn't for me. I didn't want a job where you had to work with other people.

I don't think there is one moment when you realize, This is it, this is who I am, what has just happened to me is going to change my life forever. Instead there are a series of life-altering moments, beginning when you are born and ending when you die, and a great many of these seem to occur in your teenage years.

The Skinny One

Karen Rivers

I was always the skinny one. It is my role in this family. I have two sisters. Diane is the oldest one, far enough away in age to be separate, other. She is at university, in a different world. Sonja is the middle one, eighteen months older than me, one grade ahead. She is direct and immediate competition. Here are her roles: *the pretty one, the popular one, the one who gets in trouble.* She is also the fat one. But there is some blurring of that line now, because Sonja is beginning to fade away. She has been on a diet since the seventh grade, but suddenly it is working. She eats rice cakes layered over with peanut butter so thin it is translucent and then she works it off in the gym.

She is the pretty one. But I am the smart one. I am the good one. *I am the skinny one.* If she takes skinny then all I am left with is smart and good, and that is not enough. It smacks too much of nerd, of goody-goody.

I don't put anything on *my* rice cakes at all. Peanut

butter is, after all, just flavored fat and oil. I don't need it. I take a rice cake to school for lunch and eat it in front of my locker—fast, before anyone can see me and comment—leaving small pebbly crumbs on the waxed floor. I go to the cafeteria with my friends. *I've already eaten,* I tell them. *I was starving and I couldn't wait.* I buy my diet soda and sip it slowly. I watch them eat. One girl eats an apple fritter every day. She isn't skinny. *Who does she think she is?* An apple fritter! A thousand calories of fat and sugar. I hate her for eating it. I want one so badly my chest aches and my head gets light. The empty sweetness of the diet soda turns over and over in my stomach. I push my chair back so quickly it falls over. I say, *I have to go to the library. I forgot.* I hurry away, head down, heart pounding, my mouth sore from craving so strongly what I am not allowed to have.

Not *allowed*. Says who? Me. I won't allow it.

The Popularity Plan

Aislinn Hunter

Grade 9

How it looked to everyone else

A crowd of girls, in the requisite kilts and blouses, are walking from one side of our high school campus to the other. They move in that golden kind of slow motion reserved for girl-gets-guy teen movies: kilts swish, hair is flipped casually over shoulders, textbooks are held in the crooks of their arms. When they reach the street, cars stop to let them pass. One of the girls, Kate, lowers her chin and winks at the male driver who's waving her across. She's like something out of a skin-care commercial—big smile, white teeth, perfect complexion, blonde highlights in light-brown hair. Over by the parking lot a few grade twelve basketball all-stars are watching the girls. They're leaning against a sporty green Alfa Romeo, and when they see the girls looking, they wave. Debbie, a girl with dark hair in long braids, rolls her eyes, waves back. Then the girls carry on. All eight of them, the sun shining down on them as they enter the doors of St. Anne's Secondary, heading in for class.

How it looked to me
Kate is bulldozing her way across campus with all of us in tow. I'm trying to keep up. It's spring, and the gang has dressed for it—Esprit blouses tucked into kilts, a short-sleeved Guess button-down on Caroline, Debbie in a crew-neck Ralph Lauren. The kilt and cardigan are part of the mandatory uniform, but we can wear whatever kind of white top we want. I hold my books in front of me like a shield. Under my cardigan I'm wearing a big Hanes T-shirt I took out of my brother's closet. It hangs down over the pleats of my kilt, making me look as large as a semi. I'm obviously "the fat one." And my hair is too short to flip. Walking en masse, we head across the road. Kate is talking about next week's party at Caroline and Christy's house. Who to invite, who to avoid. I listen in.

Over by the parking lot, some of the grade twelve guys wave in our direction. They're always hanging around our lockers and inviting us to after-game parties, even though we're only in grade nine. Next year all the girls I'm walking with will go to the prom, although we'll still be two years away from being seniors. Not me, though. I won't get asked. That kind of thing is a given.

Good in a Group

Anne Fleming

Twelve

In the dining room, filling out the forms that will match me up with a kid from Quebec for my pending *visite interprovinciale,* my mother and I have a big fight. You have to put a tick next to "outgoing" or "reserved." Mom insists I am reserved. I say I'm outgoing. In fact, both are true. I'm socially outgoing and emotionally reserved, though I don't have the wherewithal at age twelve to make that distinction. Mom wins the fight, as she usually does. I end up with a painfully shy and awkward girl with whom I have nothing in common. Describing her later to friends, I slap a thumb-and-forefinger L to my forehead and say "Loser!" But that's not the point here.

The point here is about being socially outgoing but emotionally reserved. This means a number of things for my friendships: 1) They tend to be less about the exchange of intimacies than the exchange of jokes; 2) They start in the public sphere—in class, in the halls, at band rehearsal, in the showers after swim practice, on the way to track meets, on ski team road trips—and stay there unless the other person initiates. Calling people up and asking them to do things makes me feel like a porcupine with its belly exposed. Bad enough to reveal you like someone, but to reveal you presume they might like you too? Aaaaaah. Too vulnerable, too vulnerable; 3) I am good in a group.

I love groups. Yeah, they can be exclusionary and dangerous, cliquey and inwardly conformist and yada yada, but even so they can be fabulous. And then there are the moments of true groupness, those rare but exquisite times when it feels everyone is equal and respected and liked, when it's clear you're all wonderful, inventive, funny people and that you're in this together, whatever *this* is.

CERTAIN THINGS ABOUT MY MOTHER

MELANIE LITTLE

Once my mother threw a ten-pound toy truck, steel, at my dad's head. Her mother, my grandma, was the same. When I was a kid, Grandma would watch calmly as I yanked down her curtains, tore out treasures from her drawers and cupboards, and turned her immaculate house upside down to construct pirate forts, supermarket displays, labyrinthine Batgirl caves. But when my grandpa came home and dripped tiny drops of mud onto the carpet, she'd chase him around in a froth, swinging a frying pan at his head.

My mom maintains that her own grandmother died of spontaneous combustion, that one morning she suddenly burst into flames and perished. I used to think this was a joke. But more and more, I figure Great-Grandma Major just got really mad at something. I can imagine the quick heating of her flesh, the burnt smell of her hair, a loud *pop*. I can believe, when it comes right down to it, anything about the women in my family.

The kids at school don't talk about their mothers much. Maybe the subject is uncool. Maybe they're like me, loaded up with fresh anecdotes every morning but swallowing them all down with massive effort, forever biting their tongues. It's true that when people's mothers *do* make a narrative appearance, it's usually to be mad about something. "My mo-om was sooo pissed," someone will say. Usually, the person is talking about getting caught at some outrageous exploit that would cause *my* mother to jump screaming off a cliff with me in tow, like necking with their pants off or stealing the answers to an exam or snorting crystal meth in the bathroom at school. Given these crimes, "sooo pissed" seems like the coolest, most enviable of understatements. Most parents would probably kill to have a goody-two-shoes kid like me — my mother even says so herself in her more pro-Melanie moods. I really believe this, I guess, that I am God's gift to parenthood, and that's what makes her rages so hard to take.

It's confusing. I have to admit that the few big things I've done have scarcely made my mother blink. I've failed tests, stolen and promptly ruined her best clothes, come home smelling like a distillery while insisting I've been at the library. I even quit figure skating after my parents had invested ten years of their lives and all of their money in it. And there was my mom, telling me she understood, she was young once, I am still the best daughter in the whole wide world. No, it's things like me leaving crumbs on the counter or asking, well in advance, if I can accept a rare and crucial invitation to go out to a movie on a school night: these are the things that have the power to light her spark and send her — both of us — up into the ether.